CABINS AND COTTAGES

TIME
LIFE ®
BOOKS

Other Publications:

PLANET EARTH
COLLECTOR'S LIBRARY OF THE CIVIL WAR
LIBRARY OF HEALTH
CLASSICS OF THE OLD WEST
THE EPIC OF FLIGHT
THE GOOD COOK
THE SEAFARERS
THE ENCYCLOPEDIA OF COLLECTIBLES
THE GREAT CITIES
WORLD WAR II
THE WORLD'S WILD PLACES
THE TIME-LIFE LIBRARY OF BOATING
HUMAN BEHAVIOR
THE ART OF SEWING
THE OLD WEST
THE EMERGENCE OF MAN
THE AMERICAN WILDERNESS
THE TIME-LIFE ENCYCLOPEDIA OF GARDENING
LIFE LIBRARY OF PHOTOGRAPHY
THIS FABULOUS CENTURY
FOODS OF THE WORLD
TIME-LIFE LIBRARY OF AMERICA
TIME-LIFE LIBRARY OF ART
GREAT AGES OF MAN
LIFE SCIENCE LIBRARY
THE LIFE HISTORY OF THE UNITED STATES
TIME READING PROGRAM
LIFE NATURE LIBRARY
LIFE WORLD LIBRARY
FAMILY LIBRARY:
   HOW THINGS WORK IN YOUR HOME
   THE TIME-LIFE BOOK OF THE FAMILY CAR
   THE TIME-LIFE FAMILY LEGAL GUIDE
   THE TIME-LIFE BOOK OF FAMILY FINANCE

This volume is part of a series offering homeowners
detailed instructions on repairs, construction
and improvements they can undertake themselves.

HOME REPAIR
AND IMPROVEMENT

CABINS AND COTTAGES

BY THE EDITORS OF
TIME-LIFE BOOKS

TIME-LIFE BOOKS
ALEXANDRIA, VIRGINIA

HOME REPAIR AND IMPROVEMENT

Editor   William Frankel
Designer   Anne Masters

Editorial Staff for Cabins and Cottages
Picture Editor   Adrian G. Allen
Text Editors   Bob Menaker, Russell B. Adams Jr.,
                                 Richard Flanagan, Lee Hassig, John Manners,
                                 Mark M. Steele, David Thiemann
Writers   Lynn R. Addison, Megan Barnett, Stephen Brown,
                                 Alan Epstein, Steven J. Forbis, Leslie Marshall,
                                 Brooke Stoddard, William Worsley
Assistant Designer   Kenneth E. Hancock
Copy Coordinator   Margery duMond
Art Assistants   George Bell, Lorraine D. Rivard, Richard Whiting
Picture Coordinator   Renée DeSandies
Editorial Assistant   Susanne S. Trice

Editorial Operations

Production Director   Feliciano Madrid
Assistants   Peter A. Inchauteguiz, Karen A. Meyerson
Copy Processing   Gordon E. Buck
Quality Control Director   Robert L. Young
Assistant   James J. Cox
Associates   Daniel J. McSweeney, Michael G. Wight
Art Coordinator   Anne B. Landry
Copy Room Director   Susan Galloway Goldberg
Assistants   Celia Beattie, Ricki Tarlow

Correspondents: Elisabeth Kraemer (Bonn); Margot
Hapgood, Dorothy Bacon, Lesley Coleman (London);
Susan Jonas, Lucy T. Voulgaris (New York); Maria
Vincenza Aloisi, Josephine du Brusle (Paris); Ann
Natanson (Rome). Valuable assistance was also
provided by: Karin B. Pearce (London); Carolyn T.
Chubet, Miriam Hsia, Christina Lieberman (New York);
Mimi Murphy (Rome).

THE CONSULTANTS: Louis Zapata, a master carpenter, has managed a construction company and supervised the design and execution of a variety of small-scale structures. He is a specialist in the renovation and restoration of old houses, most recently with the Neighborhood Housing Service, a nonprofit rehabilitation organization in Washington, D.C.

D. Duncan Joy, an engineer, has over 25 years of experience in construction design and management and is senior vice president of a structural engineering firm in northern Virginia.

Roswell W. Ard is a consulting structural engineer and a professional home inspector in northern Michigan. He has written professional papers on wood-frame construction techniques.

Harris Mitchell, a special consultant for Canada, has worked in the field of home repair and improvement for more than two decades. He is Homes editor of Today magazine and author of a syndicated newspaper column, "You Wanted to Know," as well as a number of books on home improvement.

For information about any Time-Life book, please write:
Reader Information
Time-Life Books
541 North Fairbanks Court
Chicago, Illinois 60611

Library of Congress Cataloguing in Publication Data
Time-Life Books.
    Cabins and cottages.
    (Home repair and improvement; v. 15)
    Includes index.
    1. Log cabins.   2. Cottages. I. Title.
TH4840.T55   1978   690'.8'7   78-24577
ISBN 0-8094-2412-6
ISBN 0-8094-2411-8 lib. bdg.
ISBN 0-8094-2410-X retail ed.

Contents

Getting Away from It All

Clearing the land. The hard job of moving logs on a building site is made easy by a comealong, a hand tool with a ratchet mechanism that reels in a steel cable. A chain is looped around the log and hooked to the cable, a second chain (not shown) links the other end of the comealong to a tree and the handle of the comealong is moved back and forth to pull the log toward the tree.

Small cabins and cottages are often built by amateurs. In fact, a weekend retreat—whether a fishing shack or a large A-frame with a built-in sleeping loft—is the kind of building you are most likely to tackle on your own. The techniques are not as complex nor the materials as costly as those needed for a year-round house, yet a simple, well-designed structure will prove sturdy enough for years of weekend and vacation use.

The chapters of this book follow four stages in the planning and building of a cabin of your choice. Stage One is laying a foundation, chosen to fit both the building site and the structure to be supported. The second stage involves constructing the building itself, whatever the style or size. Both the foundation and the building may have to be modified to solve special problems of terrain or climate—a job so important that it constitutes a stage in itself. And in the final stage the cabin is fitted with basic amenities—a water supply, a waste-disposal system, a source of heat.

At every stage, the key to success is simplicity. Any of the structures in this book can be converted into full-time residences, but a structure built as simply as the law permits enhances the pleasure of getting back to nature. In many remote parts of the United States and Canada, building codes are nonexistent or lightly enforced, and you can put in a foundation and put up a cabin without a permit. Elsewhere, an increasing effort is being made to extend enforcement of the Uniform Building Code, even in areas where violations were once ignored or winked at, but if you follow sound building practices, you will find that most rural building inspectors allow some leeway for buildings intended for less than full-time use.

Just as you do not need a structure that will endure for the ages in order to be comfortable in the country, you can enjoy your vacation without many of the taken-for-granted luxuries of city and suburban life. You do not need electric light at the flick of a switch, or hot and cold running water, or even a flush toilet. Light and heat can be supplied by kerosene lanterns and a wood-burning stove; you can build an outdoor privy or use a chemical toilet; and you can have running water almost anywhere without a maze of plumbing pipes and fixtures. A refrigerator, the one modern appliance you may not want to do without, can be run on bottled gas. And unless you plan to spend the winter in your cabin, you need not insulate or sheathe interior walls and ceilings.

The one element that you must accept much as you find it is the land on which you build, and the choice of a building site calls for special care. In your hunt for land, take along camping equipment: most sellers will let you stay for a day or two at the site to get the feel of the land (and the equipment will come in handy later for weekend work on the location). If possible, visit a site several times to see it at its best and worst. An apparently perfect spot, with rolling hills and a gentle creek, may show its true nature in bad weather, with the hills channeling water to the place you wanted to build on, and the creek a rampaging river after a rainstorm. If you check the site under all conditions and still like it, consider other factors:

Are access roads passable all year, are they wide enough for a truck and are they legally open to you? Widening a road or building culverts under it will add considerable expense. If you have to pass through a neighbor's property to get to your site, make sure you have or can get an easement, or right of passage.

Is water readily available and is it safe to drink? A well on adjacent property is no guarantee of water on your site. Look for other clues. For example, the presence of deep-rooted plants, such as arrowweed, mesquite, elderberry and rabbit brush, generally indicates ground water within 20 to 30 feet of the surface. If necessary, call in a professional well driller, who can give you an appraisal of the likelihood of water and the cost of reaching it—and may refund all or part of the appraisal fee if you hire him to drill the well.

Drinkable surface water from a stream, lake or pond is easy to tap, but make sure you can use it legally. In some states, mostly east of the Mississippi, you can tap any body of water that touches your property—but you may not divert all of it. In many western states, however, the first user can take all the water he wants, even if he dams it to exclude all the people downstream.

If a property meets all your requirements—and the price is right—have an accurate survey map made and a title search done to be sure the property is free and clear, before you buy it. With deed in hand, you can start turning visions of a weekend retreat into reality.

Before you begin work, make a list of the tools and materials you will need—nothing is more frustrating than the lack of a tool at a remote site. In many rural areas, you can buy lumber from a local sawmill at a real saving over the cost of buying it in the city. Wherever you buy your building supplies, you will need a small truck or van to get them to your site. For work on walls and roofs, you can rent collapsible metal scaffolding; for foundation work, you may have to rent a small, gasoline-powered concrete mixer. Nearly indispensable power tools at the site include an electric drill—⅜- or ½-inch for heavy jobs—and a circular saw; if no power lines are nearby, you will need a generator *(opposite)* to run such tools.

You can clear fairly level land yourself; grading is generally a job for a professional. With a gasoline-powered chain saw, you can fell trees as much as 40 or 50 feet tall almost as easily as you section a log for firewood, and with a lightweight hand tool called a comealong *(page 13)* you can move the felled trees around or off the site.

Generating Your Own Power

Electrically operated tools are indispensable for constructing a vacation home. If can be switched from 120-volt to supply the 240-volt current necessary to run most submersible pumps. Many can be modified to run on bottled gas, a convenience in a permanent installation. And a generator with an electric starter can be fitted with a switch that starts the pump whenever water is needed. A similarly equipped generator supplying up to 7,000 watts can operate additional electric devices such as lights and a refrigerator.

Generators are rugged, reliable devices made for hard outdoor use. The alternator needs almost no attention, although electrical contact brushes wear out eventually. (Some units feature brushless alternators for virtually trouble-free operation.) The engine requires the same attention as that of a lawn mower: periodic replenishment and replacement of the crankcase oil and a new spark plug occasionally. For safety and reliable operation, store gasoline in an approved container kept sealed when not in use.

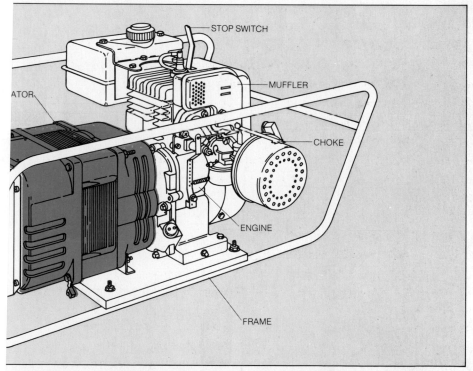

includes handles for carrying the generator. If necessary, the muffler shown here can be replaced with a spark-arresting muffler, a safety feature required by law in some localities. Almost all maintenance problems for such a unit arise in

alternator in the middle and an outlet box fitted with electrical receptacles at the other end. All three components are bolted to a frame that

the engine section. If the engine runs but the alternator produces no electricity, check the circuit breakers—located on the bottom of the outlet box of this unit—or the fuses, and reset or replace them if necessary.

Turning Untamed Land into a Building Site

Clearing a building site of underbrush, trees and rocks is mostly a matter of picking the right tool for each part of the job and using the tool simply and safely.

Cut bushes down to ground level with a pair of pruning shears and dig the roots out of the soil with a shovel. Clear tall grass and vines from the site with a scythe or hand sickle (Caution: always hold your free arm well away from the blade of a sickle). Using a drill fitted with a masonry bit, a set of steel wedges and a sledge hammer, you can easily split large rocks down to small ones that can be moved. And you can cut most saplings with one or two strokes of an ax straight through the trunk.

Felling large, mature trees is a relatively complex operation, involving three or more distinct cuts. Loggers used to make these cuts with hand axes and two-man crosscut saws, but the modern gasoline-powered chain saw, used with care, has replaced ax and saw, and put the job within anyone's capacity.

Where you make the cuts to fell a large tree depends on the direction in which it is leaning. If the lean is not obvious—or if the tree may get hung up in surrounding trees—use ropes to help pull it in the desired direction. Because a chain saw is noisy and because its operation demands your full attention, have a helper stand behind you as you cut, to warn you by tapping you with a stick when the top of the tree begins to move.

Felling a slightly leaning tree calls for three cuts: two to make a notch in the face of the tree (the side closer to the ground) and a final "felling cut" on the opposite side. The cuts leave a narrow intact strip inside the trunk—loggers call this section a hinge—which holds the trunk together until the tree hits the ground, giving you time to move to safety. You can fell a slightly leaning tree away from the natural lean by changing the shape of the hinge and the position of the notch and then driving wedges into the felling cut (page 12).

Extra care must be taken when felling a tree that leans more than 20° because the wood opposite the direction of lean is almost always brittle and may split and fly up at you as you make the felling cut. Loggers call the result a "barber chair" because the remaining cut and broken half trunk resembles a seat with a slanting back. To prevent a barber chair, hook a chain around the tree and make special side cuts (page 12).

When you have felled a tree, cut off any spring poles—branches or nearby saplings bent under the tree when it landed—so they will not snap back at you when you cut the tree into sections. Then trim the exposed limbs and remove the tree with the hauling device called a comealong (page 13).

The Safe Way to Fell a Tree

1 Anchoring the tree. To ensure that a tree falls in the right direction, anchor the trunk to trees located at a distance at least twice the height of the tree. Tie two 1-inch ropes to the tree as high on the trunk as you can safely reach, then tie the other ends of the ropes around the bases of the anchoring trees.

If there are no trees you can use as anchors, you can make what loggers call a holdfast (inset). Drive two wooden pickets—5 feet long and at least 3 inches thick—3 feet into the ground, leaning away from the tree you will fell. Nail a 2-by-4 between the top of the picket nearer the tree and the bottom of the other picket. Tie the anchoring rope low on the first picket.

2 **Making the notch cuts.** On the face of the tree—the side on the direction of the lean—make a horizontal cut a third of the way into the trunk, and a second cut from above it to meet the first at a 45° angle. If the saw binds, free it with wooden or plastic wedges driven into the cut with a mallet. Knock out the wedge-shaped section you have cut in the tree.

3 **Making the felling cut.** On the opposite side of the trunk, make a horizontal cut 2 inches above the horizontal notch cut, stopping the blade 2 to 3 inches from the back of the notch. If the tree does not begin to fall, start it by driving wedges into the felling cut.

Have a helper ready to tap you with a stick when the tree begins to fall so you can turn off the chain saw and retreat to safety along an escape route. The best route is along a line 135° back from the direction of the tree's lean.

A Deep Cut in Easy Stages

To fell a large tree—up to twice as thick as the length of the chain-saw blade—you must make two or more felling cuts. Make the notch cut as in Step 2 at left. Then start the first felling cut, holding your body stationary and swinging the saw *(below, top)*. To make the succeeding felling cuts, place the edge of the saw at the end of the preceding cut and walk the blade around the tree *(below, bottom)*. Leave a 2-inch hinge between the felling cuts and the notch cut just as you would for a smaller tree.

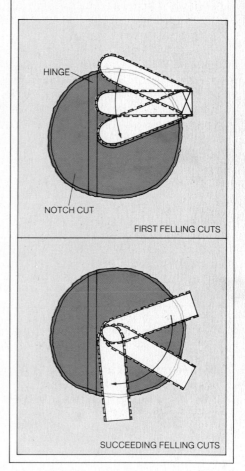

HINGE

NOTCH CUT

FIRST FELLING CUTS

SUCCEEDING FELLING CUTS

FELLING CUT

HINGE

NOTCH CUT

DIRECTION OF FALL

ESCAPE ROUTE

Special Problems in the Lean of a Tree

Felling a deeply leaning tree. Bind the tree with a heavy chain about 3 feet above the ground, then make a shallow cut on each side of the tree a foot below the chain (*inset*) to prevent the tree from splitting along a line between the brittle wood at the back and the dense wood at the face. Make notch cuts halfway into the trunk at the same level as the side cuts, then make the felling cut as you would for a tree that has only a moderate lean.

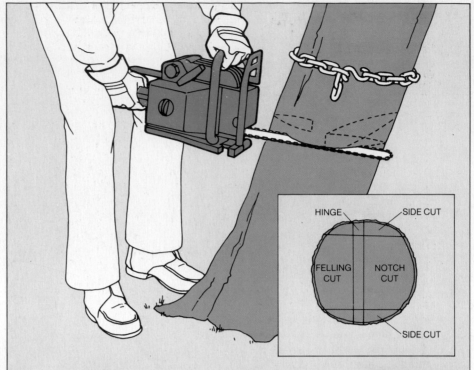

HINGE — SIDE CUT

FELLING CUT — NOTCH CUT

SIDE CUT

Felling away from the lean. Make the notch cuts on the side where you want the tree to fall and angle the felling cut so the thick part of the hinge is opposite the natural direction of lean (*near right*).

Drive wooden or plastic wedges into the felling cut near the thin side of the hinge (*far right*). The wedges will force the tree upward on that side (*inset*), shifting its center of gravity away from the lean. If the wedges do not cause the tree to fall, deepen the felling cut.

DIRECTION OF FALL

LEAN

THICK END

THIN END

Removing Logs, Stumps and Boulders

You can maneuver logs and large stones around your building site and remove tree stumps easily without the use of heavy machinery. The simplest tool for moving logs, first used by 19th Century loggers, is the peavey, a wooden shaft fitted with a metal point and hinged hook that dig into the log you are rolling along the ground. Though not widely available, peaveys are still sold by some tool-specialty stores. More readily available—it is sold at most large hardware stores—is the comealong, a hand tool with a ratchet mechanism and a lever that is moved back and forth to reel in a cable or chain. Buy a heavy-duty model capable of pulling at least a ton—enough to handle the heaviest tree or section of tree you are likely to have to move.

After you have moved the trees off your site, cut the stumps to within a foot of the ground. If you plan to build on the site immediately, have a professional blast the stumps or grind them down with a gasoline-powered stump grinder. A slower but simpler way to remove a stump is to burn it away with chemicals sold for the purpose by most hardware stores and garden centers. After five or six weeks, when the chemicals have saturated the stump, you can burn it off to the roots. Check with local fire authorities before you burn the stump: during periods of dry weather, such burning may not be permitted.

To move a large rock, break it down to movable size—less than 300 pounds—by drilling into it with a carbide-tipped masonry bit and driving steel wedges into the holes until the rock splits. Then twist malleable iron wire around the rock so you can hook a comealong to it.

Dragging a log with a comealong. Attach one log chain to the log, 2 feet from the end, and a second chain to a nearby tree. Hook the movable cable of the comealong to the chain around the log and hook the stationary end to the chain on the tree; draw the log toward the tree by moving the handle of the comealong back and forth. A release (*inset*) frees the handle.

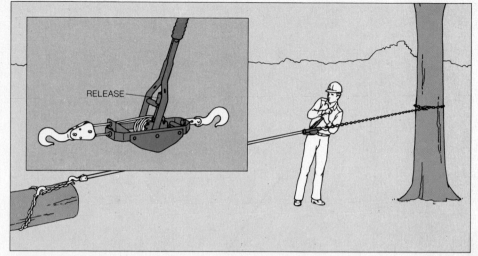

RELEASE

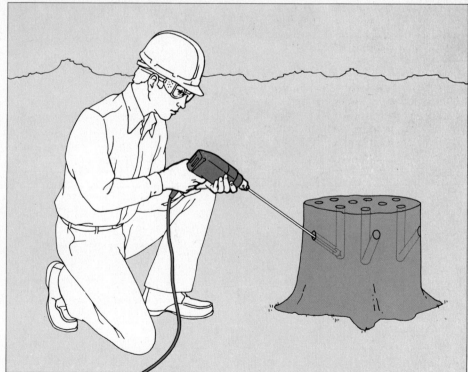

Attacking a stump with chemicals. Drill 1-inch vertical holes 10 inches into the stump, no more than 6 inches apart; 4 inches from the top of the stump, drill diagonally into the vertical holes. Fill the holes three fourths full with flammable chemicals and add water to the top. When the water and chemicals have been absorbed, refill the holes with chemicals and nail a sheet of plastic over the stump. Dig a firebreak 18 inches deep around the stump, with its inner edge about 4 feet from the stump.

After five to six weeks, remove the plastic and fill the holes with kerosene. Place pieces of charcoal on the stump, soak the charcoal with kerosene and light it—the stump will smoulder up to 24 hours before it is reduced to ashes. Caution: if you must leave the site, extinguish the fire.

Pin-point Foundations on Poles and Piers

From a distance, a cottage resting upon wooden poles or masonry piers may look shaky and fragile. In reality, such a foundation can hold its own through storms and floods. It cannot be used everywhere; in some localities building codes require the continuous-wall foundations shown on pages 26-31, and foundation walls are preferred in earthquake-prone areas and in cold climates. But wherever they can be used, poles and piers make a practical and attractive alternative to a walled foundation; because they call for less material and labor, they save both money and time.

The building techniques on these pages are designed for level sites and stable soil. (Uneven terrain and insecure soils, such as soft clay or loose sand, call for somewhat different methods, described on pages 80-85.) These techniques are versatile—with slight modifi-

cations, they will serve for wooden or concrete poles and for concrete-block or precast-concrete piers. Of all these materials, the simplest and easiest to put up are the wooden poles shown below.

At your lumber dealer, order poles 6 to 8 inches thick and especially designed for use in house construction; such poles generally come treated with an oil- or water-base preservative that will protect the wood from insects and rot and will not harm vegetation. Before the poles are delivered, inspect them yourself to be sure that they are fairly straight and uniform in diameter.

After laying out the boundaries of the cottage (pages 26-27, Steps 1 and 2), locate the corner and intermediate side poles, as well as the interior poles. Poles generally are spaced 8 feet apart. Their height above the ground can range from 1½ to 3 feet, but they must be sunk at

least 4 feet into the earth for stability.

Digging such holes is easy if you use a gasoline-powered auger, available from tool-rental centers in models for one or two operators. When you have dug the holes and braced the poles in them, you must encase each pole in a jacket of either concrete or a wet mixture of 1 part cement to 5 parts clean soil, free of roots, leaves and other decomposable matter (the consistency of the mixture should be that of concrete, but the amount of water will vary, depending on the soil). The jacket, which fills the hole completely, increases the pole's effective diameter in the earth.

After the poles are firmly embedded in the ground, floor beams are clamped into shallow notches, called daps, cut in the sides of each pole. From that point, for every type of pole or pier, the job consists of installing joists and a floor.

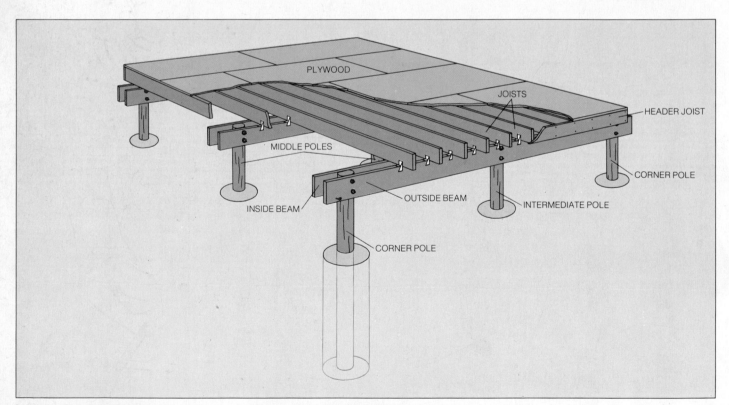

PLYWOOD

JOISTS

HEADER JOIST

MIDDLE POLES

CORNER POLE

OUTSIDE BEAM

INTERMEDIATE POLE

INSIDE BEAM

CORNER POLE

Anatomy of a pole platform. The foundation above consists of three rows of poles sunk into the ground at 8-foot intervals. Below ground, each pole is firmly secured by a jacket of soil-cement mixture; aboveground, the poles are sandwiched between 2-by-10 beams, fastened in place with threaded rods, washers and nuts. Floor joists are fastened to the outside beams and to a middle beam by means of hardware called framing anchors, and to header joists with nails.

In this example sheets of plywood, which can serve as either a subfloor or a finish floor, have been laid to cover the entire platform.

Putting Up a Pole Platform

1 Digging the holes. With the locations of the poles marked and the boundary strings *(page 26)* removed, use a power auger to dig pole holes to a depth of 4 feet, raising the bit slowly every few inches to clear dirt from the hole; if your building code calls for a deeper hole, fit the auger with an extension bit. Use hand tools to widen the holes to a diameter 10 to 12 inches larger than that of the posts. Set all the poles in place, the straightest and largest at the corners.

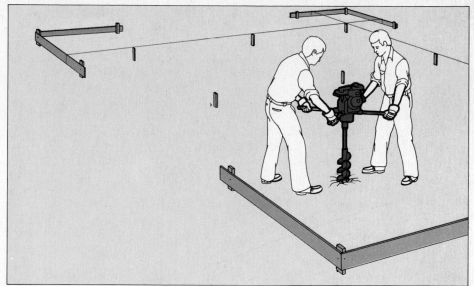

2 Lining up the poles. Plumb the corner poles and brace them with stakes and lengths of scrap wood; then stretch a horizontal string fitted with a line level along the outside faces of the corner poles and align the intermediate poles against the string. After plumbing and bracing these poles, measure up from the string along each outside row and mark the levels for the bottoms of the outside beams. Repeat the process for the middle poles; the end poles of this row need not align exactly with the corner poles, but the row itself should be perfectly straight. Make a jacket for each pole, overfilling the hole slightly and grading the top of the jacket down from the pole to the surface. Let the jacket cure for one day.

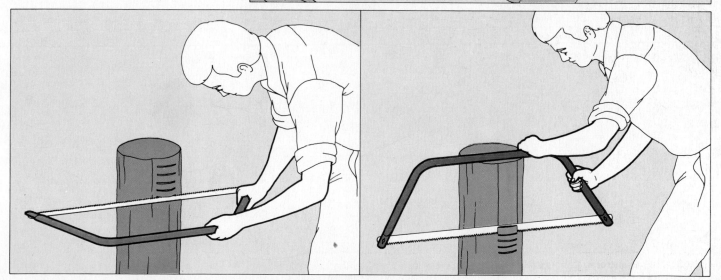

3 Cutting daps for the first beams. On the outside of the end rows and on either side of the middle row, make daps, or recesses, for a set of beams in the following way. Using a pruning saw or a bucksaw, make a series of horizontal cuts, each about 1½ inches wide and from ⅛ to ¼ inch deep, down from the top of a pole to the mark for the bottom of a beam *(above, left)*. Complete the dap by making a vertical saw cut *(above, right)* as deep as the horizontal ones.

4 **Attaching the beams.** Set a beam against the daps in each row of poles, check to be sure it is level, then fasten it in place with a nail driven partway into each pole. If possible, use beams that are long enough to span a complete row of poles. Otherwise lap shorter beams by a foot at the pole in the center of a row and install spacer blocks between the ends of the offset beams and the end poles.

Cut off the tops of the poles to a level flush with the top edges of the beams.

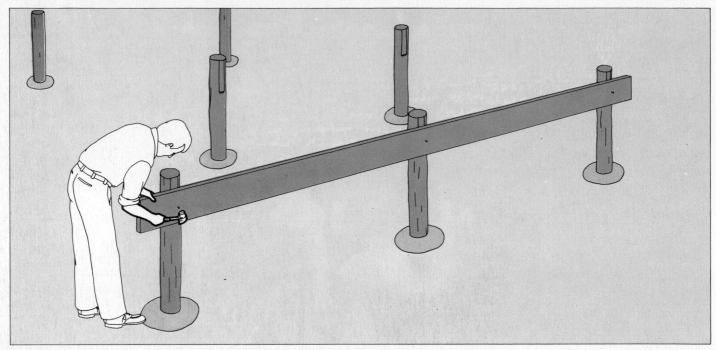

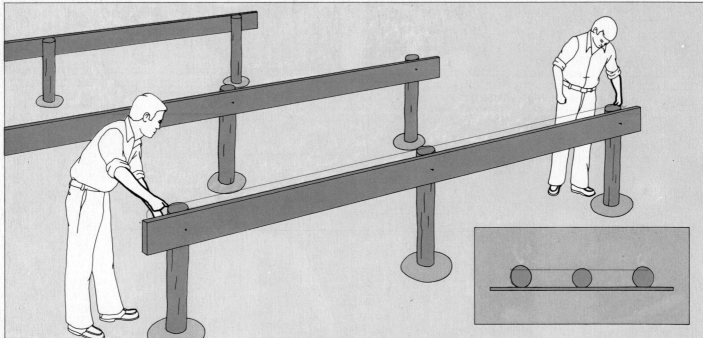

5 **Attaching the second set of beams.** Stretch a string over each row of poles opposite the installed beam, with at least 1½ inches of string over each pole (inset). Mark the string's path over the poles, cut daps at the marks—you may have to cut especially deep daps in one or two poles—and loosely fasten the remaining beams.

6 **Bolting the beams.** One third of the way from the bottom and the top of each beam, drill ½-inch holes completely through the beam-pole-beam sandwich; pour a commercial preservative into each hole, then run threaded bolt rods through the holes. Secure the assembly with washers and nuts on both sides and apply shellac to the exposed metal to prevent rust.

Check the nuts for tightness several weeks after the foundation is completed: beams and poles may shrink slightly with exposure on the site.

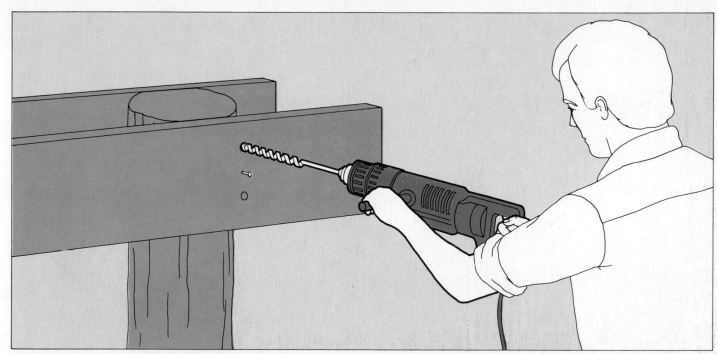

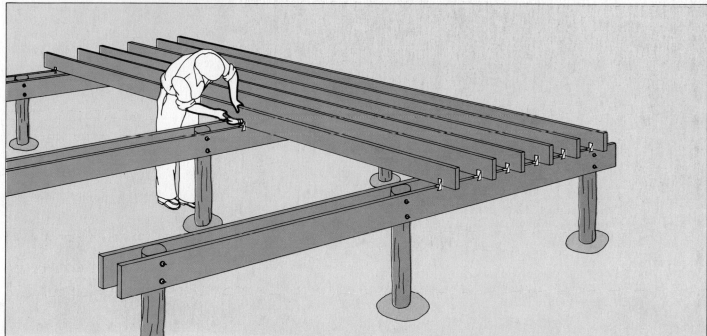

7 **Attaching the joists.** Set the joists across the beams at 16-inch intervals and fasten them to the beams with framing anchors, one anchor at each pair of beams; nail header joists to the open ends of the main joists to close the perimeter of the joist platform. A deck of plywood—preferably ¾-inch—completes the platform.

Masonry for Stronger Supports

Piers make a more durable masonry foundation than wooden poles, and are almost as easy to put up. You can make them in three different ways: by pouring concrete into cylindrical fiber forms; by stacking and mortaring masonry-block piers and filling the cores of the blocks with concrete; or by simply setting precast piers of solid concrete.

Each method has advantages and disadvantages. Cylindrical molds can be poured to any height, making it easy to set the tops of the piers to the same level. Blocks are the cheapest, but leveling must be done during excavation of the pier bases to make the height come out right. Precast concrete piers are the simplest to install, but they are heavy (90 to 150 pounds) and therefore awkward to transport and set into position. Like masonry blocks, they must be set on level bases, and because they generally come no more than 18 inches high, they are used mainly on level sites that have a shallow frost line.

All three types of piers rest on footings, solid concrete bases that sit at a depth specified by the local code and are wide and thick enough to carry the weight of the structures above them. In general, a footing should be as thick as the width of a pier, and twice as wide—a pier 8 inches wide, for example, would require a footing 8 inches thick and 16 inches wide.

To level the footings for block piers, use a water level (opposite, below) to mark a fixed height on all the vertical reinforcing rods, then measure down from the marks to set the height of the concrete for the footings. Precast piers do not take vertical rods; to level their footings, drive stakes into the footing holes, mark the heights of the footings in the same way, pour concrete up to the marks and remove the stakes before the footing concrete begins to harden.

Materials for all three kinds of pier are available from masonry suppliers. Fiber tubes 8 inches in diameter and 10 feet long make quick work of pouring cylindrical concrete piers; store them upright and keep them perfectly dry until they are filled. Masonry blocks come in a wide range of sizes; single-core, 12-by-12-by-8-inch blocks make particularly sturdy piers. Both cylinders and masonry-block piers must be fitted with hardware to secure the girders or beams that will support the floor (the drawings on page 21 show a typical example); precast piers are generally sold with nailing anchors or strips already embedded in them.

Pouring Your Own Piers

1 **Setting a vertical rod.** Dig each footing hole 16 inches wide (twice the width of the pier) and at least 8 inches deeper than the depth of the pier below ground. At the center of the hole, drive a length of reinforcing rod into the ground until the top of the rod is about 6 inches below the planned height of the pier aboveground. Set four bricks around the rod, halfway between the base of the rod and the bottom rim of the hole.

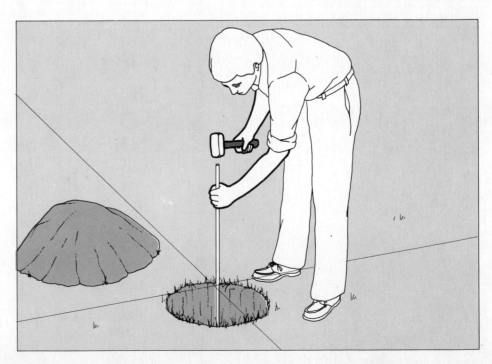

2 Pouring the footing. Fasten two 14-inch lengths of reinforcing rod together in the form of a cross, using a strip of tie wire that is long enough for you to make a loop over the vertical rod, and lower the crossed rods down onto the bricks. Pour a concrete footing 8 inches deep and allow it to dry for at least one day.

3 Positioning the form. Slide the form down over the vertical reinforcing rod until it rests upon the hardened footing. Fill the hole outside the form with earth, tamping every 6 inches and plumbing the form as you go.

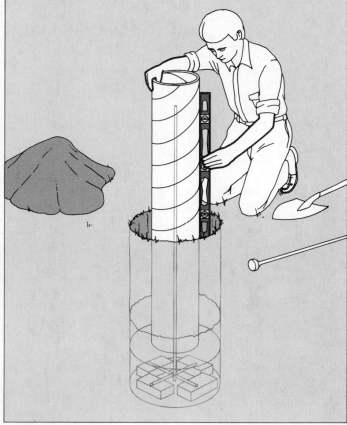

4 Leveling the forms. Mark the planned height of the piers on a corner form; then, using a water level or a transparent plastic hose almost filled with water, hold one end of the hose against the form so that the water in the hose is exactly level with the mark. Have a helper hold the other end against another form and mark this form at the level of the water. Repeat the process for each form in the foundation and cut the forms off at the marked heights.

19

5 **Setting the anchor.** Pour and tamp concrete into each form a foot at a time. When the mix is even with the top of a form, bend a framing anchor like the one shown so that the distance between the anchor's wings, or uprights, is equal to the width of a double beam—3 inches for a pair of 2-by-10s or 2-by-12s—and push the anchor into the concrete. To secure the anchor while the concrete hardens, run wire through the anchor wings and fasten the wire ends to the sides of the form. Check the alignment of each row of anchors with a string, let the concrete set for 24 hours, then remove the wire. Allow another three to seven days for the concrete to cure.

If you wish to remove the part of the form aboveground, make vertical cuts through the fiber and peel it off. The part below ground will rot away without weakening the pier.

6 **Attaching a beam.** Set the doubled beam into the anchors—if a beam is not level, shim the low end upward with galvanized washers between the beam and the pier—and fasten the beam in place with four nails driven through each anchor into the beam. Add joists and plywood to complete the platform (*page 17, Step 7*).

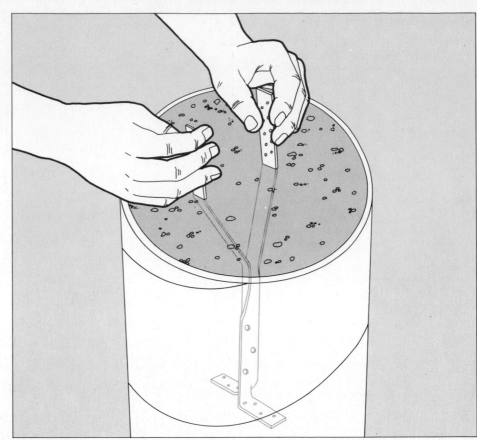

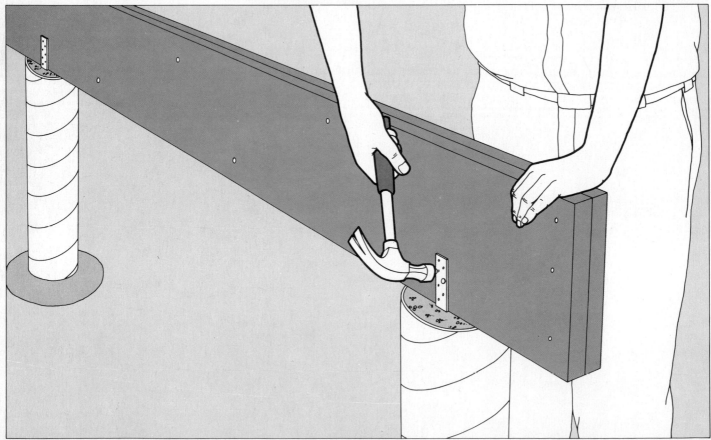

Masonry Blocks and Prefabs

A concrete-block pier. Using the strings that mark the edges of the building *(page 27)* as a guide, mark the positions of the bottom blocks for the four corner piers on the footings; spread mortar beds on the footings and lay the blocks at the marks, with the vertical reinforcing rods passing through their cores. As you bring the corner piers to their full height, use a level to keep the blocks level and plumb, and a story pole *(page 28)* to gauge the ⅜-inch mortar joints; then use a mason's line *(page 28)* strung from corner to corner to set the height and alignment of the remaining piers.

When all blocks are laid, fill the cores of the piers with concrete and embed a framing anchor in each pier *(opposite, Step 5)*.

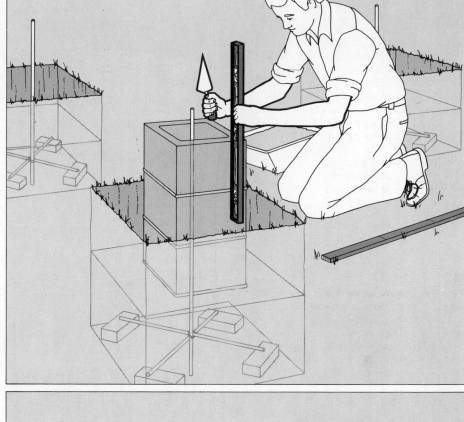

A precast-concrete pier. Mark the positions of the piers on the footings, spread full mortar beds on the footings and, with a helper, lay the piers in the mortar at the marks. Check the level of each pier in the mortar bed and, if necessary, adjust its seat in the bed. To fasten beams to the anchor shown here, drive nails through the anchor and into a prenailed double beam; other anchors are flexible enough to wrap around a beam.

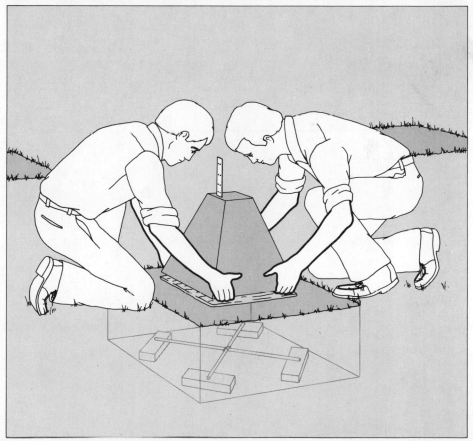

The Ease and Speed of a Wooden Foundation

Though they are still fairly novel, continuous foundation walls made of wood alone can be ideal for a lightweight cabin. The job of building such a foundation calls for no more than the basic carpentry skills. Because the foundation requires no concrete, it saves both money and the time required for concrete to harden, and it can be erected in nearly any weather.

Wooden foundations are not feasible in some locations. In hot, moist climates where dry rot and termites are serious problems, even the best methods of protecting or preserving wood have a limited usefulness. Furthermore, certain soils, such as clay or silt, are unsuitable, due to poor drainage and load-bearing capacities. And, perhaps because they are un-usual, wooden foundations are not yet approved by many building codes.

If practical or legal limitations do not prevent you from putting in a wooden foundation, you may well choose one for its simplicity and speed of construction. The typical crawl-space foundation illustrated here, for example, can be built in a weekend by two workers. It consists of framed and sheathed panels similar to those on pages 36-43, made of pressure-treated lumber and plywood and joined together with hot-dipped zinc nails. The panels are laid on a footing plate over a bed of washed pea gravel, in a trench dug below the frost line or, in an area of shallow frost, at least 10 inches deep.

When the panels are in place, the trench is partly filled with more pea gravel, the floor joists are installed and the rest of the trench is filled with dirt. A structure larger than 16 feet by 24 feet requires additional support for the joists, generally provided by center panels that are trenched, framed and sheathed like the wall panels. Butt the inner ends of 2-by-10 joists over this panel; for single joists, use 2-by-10s for spans up to 14 feet, 2-by-12s for spans to 16 feet.

Pea gravel can be obtained from sand-and-gravel suppliers or building-supply houses, and pressure-treated wood is available at any lumberyard. Although almost any type of lumber is suitable, check to be sure that the grade you buy will support the structure.

Anatomy of a wooden foundation. The wall panels at the heart of this crawl-space foundation rest on 2-by-8 footing plates laid over a 4-inch bed of washed gravel in a trench 12 inches wide; grade stakes embedded in the gravel are used to set the 4-inch level. The panels are framed with 2-by-6 studs, sole plates and doubled top plates, and sheathed on the outer side with ½-inch pressure-treated plywood; header and floor joists are fastened to the top plates.

In cross section (*inset*), the panel located at the right of a corner (as seen from the outside of the structure) butts against a left-corner panel, and the sheathing of the right-corner panel overlaps that of the left-corner panel.

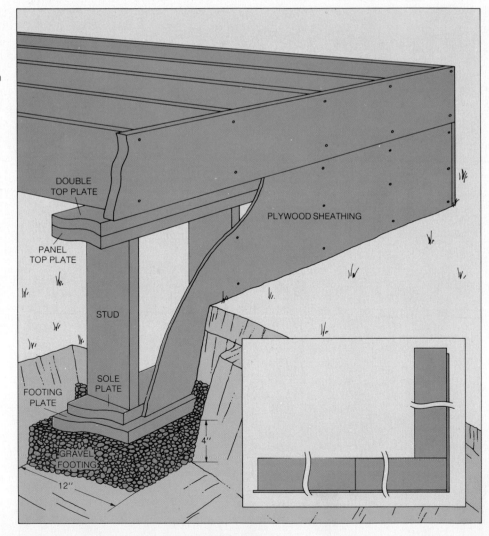

DOUBLE TOP PLATE

PANEL TOP PLATE

PLYWOOD SHEATHING

STUD

SOLE PLATE

FOOTING PLATE

GRAVEL FOOTING

4"

12"

Readying the Trench

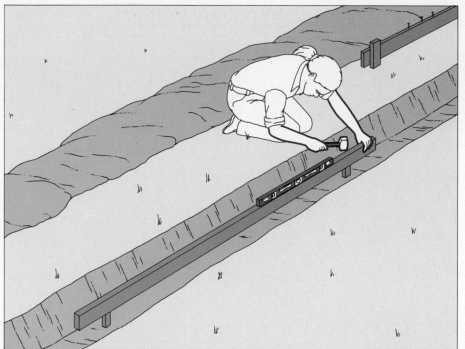

1 Setting the stakes. After digging the trench *(page 27)*, use a long straightedge and a carpenter's level to adjust the height of the grade stakes that will mark the depth of the gravel footing bed. To position the stakes, measure 3 inches in from the building lines as marked on the batter boards *(page 27)*—this will be the center line of the footing plates. Set 1-foot-long pressure-treated 2-by-2 stakes at each corner of the center line and at 7-foot intervals between the corners. Drive one corner stake down until it projects exactly 4 inches from the soil at the bottom of the trench; then, checking with the straightedge and carpenter's level, tap each succeeding stake to the same height.

2 Leveling the gravel bed. After distributing pea gravel evenly in the trench, use a leveling hoe to smooth the gravel to the height of the grade stakes. To begin this step of the job, toenail 2-by-4s on edge along the tops of the stakes to serve as a guide track for the leveling hoe (check the stakes to be sure you do not drive them below the 4-inch level; reset them if necessary). Make the hoe from a piece of ¾-inch plywood measuring 9 by 12 inches and notched to fit the guide track; attach a 2-by-2 handle braced with a length of scrap. Work the hoe with pushing and pulling movements, shaving the gravel down until the tops of the stakes are just visible, then remove the guide track.

Making and Laying Panels

1 **Framing the panels.** Drive 20-penny zinc nails through single 2-by-6 top and bottom plates and into 2-by-6 studs, each 19½ inches high. Make the eight corner panels 7½ feet wide, the middle panels—as many as are needed to complete the building—8 feet wide. Set the studs on 16-inch centers, with one short stud space at either end of a corner panel.

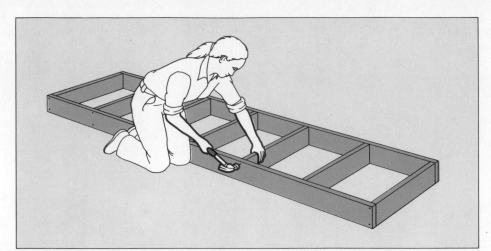

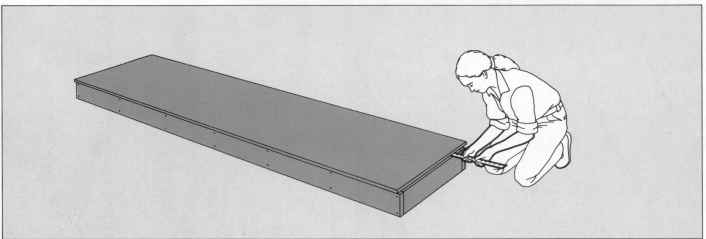

2 **Sheathing the panels.** Cover the panels with ½-inch pressure-treated plywood sheathing, fastened to the studs with eightpenny zinc nails at 6-inch intervals and cut to the following dimensions. On all panels, set the sheathing flush with the sole plate and have it overhang the top plate by 1½ inches. On an 8-foot panel, recess the sheathing by ¾ inch at the right end, as seen from the outside of the panel, and have it overhang ¾ inch at the left end. On a right-corner panel (*page 22, inset*), recess the sheathing ¾ inch at the right end and have it overhang 6 inches at the left end. On a left-corner panel, set the sheathing flush with the right end and have it overhang the left end ¾ inch.

3 **Installing the footing plates.** Place the 2-by-8 footing plates in the trench with their outer edges flush with a line stretched 1 inch outside the building line. (If you must cut the plates to fit, coat the cut ends with a commercial preservative at three to five times the concentration recommended by the manufacturer.) Drive small stakes on both sides of the plates to keep them from shifting, square the corners with a steel square, and toenail the plates together. Snap a chalk line 1 inch in from the inside edges of the plates to mark the positions of the foundation panels.

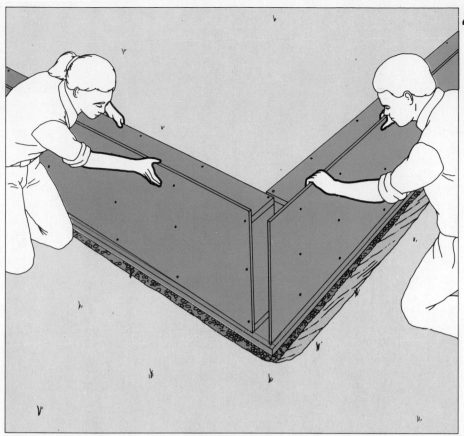

4 **Installing the panels.** Position a pair of corner panels along the chalk lines on the footing plate, fitting the end of the panel at the left of the corner (as seen from outside the structure) snugly against the 6-inch overhang of the right-corner panel. Nail the right-corner panel to the footing plate at each stud space. Move the left-corner panel slightly out of position and seal the end with butyl caulking, then set the panel along the chalk line and nail it to the footing plate. Nail the panels together at the studs.

Caulk the other end of the left-corner panel and install the next panel along the chalk line, fitting the overlaps and recesses tightly together. Proceed around the building line until all of the foundation panels are in place.

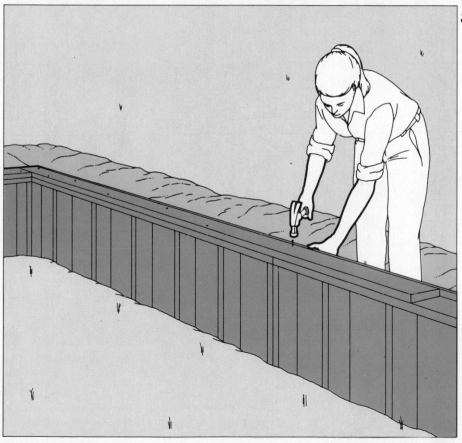

5 **Finishing the foundation.** Nail 2-by-6s to the top plate of the panels, offsetting the panel joints by 3 feet. Brace the corner panels with stakes and 2-by-4s, and fill the trench with pea gravel to within 2 feet of the corners. Install floor joists on top of the plates *(page 17)*. Use a single joist at the double studs of panel joints, and nail a 2-by-4 to the side of the joist, flush with the top, to serve as a nailing block for the subflooring. To support the ends of joists near two corners of the structure, cut extra studs and toenail them into the foundation wall. Fill the trench corners halfway to the top with pea gravel, then finish filling the trench with soil, graded down and away from the outside of the wall to a slope of ½ inch per foot for a minimum of 6 feet.

Strongest of All: A Continuous Block Wall

A continuous wall of concrete block resting on a footing of poured concrete is the most expensive foundation for a vacation home and the hardest to build—but it is the strongest, the most permanent and the most weather-tight. It may be required by a local building code; in any case it is generally necessary for heavy buildings like log cabins, for maximum protection in earthquake or hurricane country, and for unstable soil that cannot support the pin-point load of piers or poles. In other situations, the advantages outweigh the cost. In very cold country, for example, concrete block is often preferred to elevated foundations because it is easier to insulate and because a water heater and plumbing pipes can be housed in a weather-tight crawl space.

The length of each wall in a block foundation must be a multiple of 8 inches—half the length of a standard masonry block—or the walls will not fit together properly. The footings must extend at least 18 inches below ground— more where the frost line is deeper—and the walls must rise 24 inches above grade level, to protect the wooden floor and walls from moisture and termites.

To determine the number of blocks you need for the foundation walls, multiply their total length in feet by the number of courses, then by .75. The mortar can be made either from 1 part (by volume) portland cement, 1 part hydrated lime, 6 parts damp sand, and water; or by combining 1 part premixed masonry cement, 3 parts sand, and water.

If you need deep trenches for the footings, you probably will want to get a backhoe operator to dig them for you; in any case, do not try to dig deeper than 4 feet unless you have had extensive experience that will enable you to prevent dangerous cave-ins. Have dirt dumped just outside the trenches, in low mounds that will not block the chute of a concrete truck; then, after the floor joists are installed, you can backfill around the foundation wall with the same dirt.

For a project of this size, it is usually easier to have the concrete delivered in a transit-mix truck than to mix it yourself. Order one cubic yard of concrete for every 22 linear feet of footing. If possible, clear the site so the truck can back up to each side of the building and pour the concrete directly into the footings. Otherwise, assemble a group of helpers with wheelbarrows and plywood chutes.

Planning and Pouring the Footing

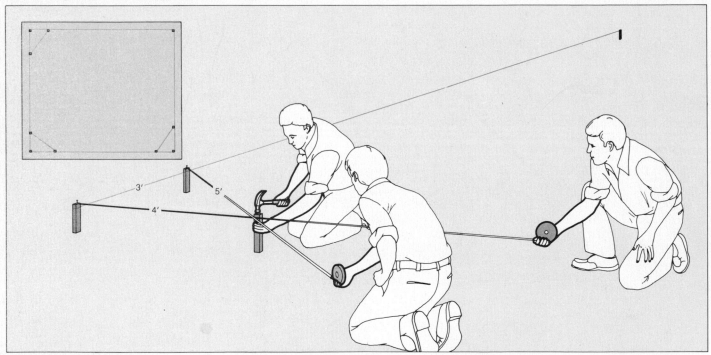

1 Laying out the building lines. With stakes and two steel tape measures lay out the outside of the foundation walls, using the 3-4-5 triangle method to get right angles at the corners. Drive stakes at two adjacent corners of the planned buildings, drive nails into the tops of the stakes and stretch a string taut between the nails to indicate one side of the building. Exactly 3 feet along the string from one corner stake, drive a measuring stake and nail. Have one helper hook a tape over that stake, and a second helper hook a tape over the corner stake; swing the tapes across each other. Where the 4-foot mark on the corner-stake tape and the 5-foot mark on the measuring-stake tape cross, drive another measuring stake. Use this stake and the corner stake to establish the second side of the building, measuring the length of the wall along a line running through the two stakes and driving the third corner stake and its nail at that point. Locate the fourth corner in the same way (inset), using the previously established corner stakes and additional measuring stakes to create a 3-4-5 right triangle (dashed lines).

For greater accuracy, you may prefer to use triangles based on multiples of 3, 4 and 5 feet— 9-12-15, for example. And to check your layout, compare the diagonal measurements between corners, which should be identical.

2 **Making and marking batter boards.** Transfer the building lines to structures called batter boards, which serve as reference points. Drive three 2-by-4 batter-board stakes about 5 feet outside each corner stake to form a right angle that matches the corner, then nail 1-by-6s 8 feet long to the three batter-board stakes. Stretch a string from a corner stake to the batter boards at an adjacent corner and move the taut string until it brushes the nail on top of the second corner stake, then mark the string's location on the top of the batter board. Repeat the procedure for the building lines at each corner.

Mark each batter board, making the first mark 7⅝ inches inside the building line for the inside of the foundation wall; mark the board 4 inches outside the building line and 12 inches inside for the footing. Mark an additional 24 inches outside the outer footing mark and 6 inches inside the inner footing mark for the edges of the trench *(inset)*. Drive nails into the batter board at each mark and remove the corner stakes.

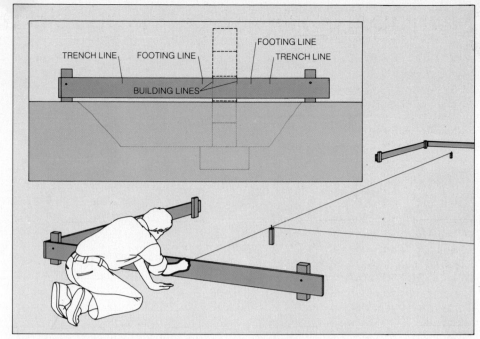

3 **Digging the trench.** Stretch strings between low stakes driven at the trench-line marks and trace the strings along the ground with a squeeze bottle of powdered chalk. Dig the trench to a depth 8 inches less than the footing depth required by code. Caution: trenches deeper than 4 feet present a cave-in hazard and are best left to professionals.

Stretch strings between footing marks on the batter boards, drop plumb lines from the strings to the bottom of the trench and mark lines for the footing trench as you did for the original excavation. Dig the trenches 8 inches deep.

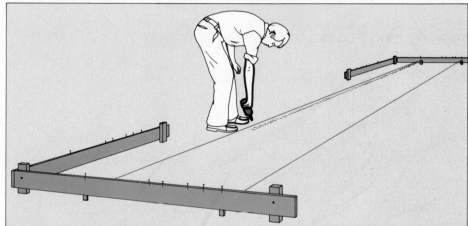

4 **Leveling the footing trench.** Drive 1-by-2 stakes at each corner of the footing trench, mark one stake 8 inches from the bottom of the trench and transfer the 8-inch mark to the other stakes with a water level. For additional reference points, drive stakes 3 inches from the sides of the trench every 3 feet, alternating from one side to the other, and transfer the marks to them. Measure down from the mark on each stake to the bottom of the trench and deepen it wherever necessary to at least 8 inches; the concrete will fill any deeper sections.

Drive 16-inch lengths of ½-inch reinforcing bar—called grade pegs—into the footing trench next to each stake until the top of each bar is level with the mark. Remove the wooden stakes and tamp the dirt around the grade pegs.

5 **Pouring a reinforced footing.** Support long pieces of No. 4 reinforcing bar about 3 inches above the bottom of the trench with bricks or stones, then lash the bars to the grade pegs with wire. Where two pieces of bar meet, overlap them about 16 inches and lash them together. To make bends in the reinforcing bar for the corners, slip a piece of iron pipe over the end of the bar, lay the bar on the ground, step on it and pull the pipe up gradually.

Pour the concrete to just above the tops of the grade pegs and work it around the reinforcing bars with a shovel, then level and smooth the concrete with a wooden float until the tops of the grade pegs barely show. Cover the footings with polyethylene sheeting and let them cure for at least 24 hours.

Stretch strings between the building-line marks on the batter boards, drop a plumb bob from each string and snap matching chalk lines on the footings. Remove the strings.

Building the Foundation Wall

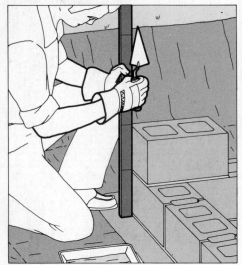

MASON'S LINE

1 **Building the leads.** At each corner of the trench, lay a stepped set of blocks called a lead. To start this part of the job, spread a mortar bed 10 inches wide and 1½ inches thick from the corner, set a corner block between the chalk lines and tap the block down with a trowel until the mortar joint is ⅜ inch thick. Check the position of the block with a mason's level.

Lay four blocks on each side of the corner, checking them with the level as you work; then spread a 1-inch bed of mortar on this course, set a corner block on top of the first one and perpendicular to it, and tap the corner block down. Check the height of the corner blocks with a story pole—a 1-by-2 marked every 8 inches to indicate the level of each course—building up or reducing the thickness of the mortar joints as necessary.

2 **Leveling the wall.** Hook a mason's line between two adjacent corners, using corner-gripping mason's blocks, and align the line precisely with the top of the first course of blocks; then spread a 1½-inch mortar bed on the footing and complete the first course of blocks. Keep the face of each block $1/16$ inch from the mason's line and the top level with the line. When you reach the centers of the two opposite walls that will support the girder—generally the shorter walls in a rectangular building—substitute a

solid block for the normal hollow-cored one. Move the mason's line up to lay the second and third courses, always using solid blocks where the ends of the girder will rest. (In these pictures, solid blocks are indicated by heavy outlines.)

Lay a mortar bed at each corner for the leads of the next three courses and press masonry-type wire-mesh reinforcement into the mortar, then lay the next three courses. Add a layer of mesh reinforcement over every third course.

3 **Venting the crawl space.** On opposite sides of the building, about 4 feet from the corners and 8 inches aboveground, omit a block to leave a space for a vent—one for every 300 square feet of floor space. Fill around the opening with mortar, set the vent 4 inches inside the wall, with its tabs atop the blocks on either side, and pack mortar around the vent edges, slanting mortar at the bottom outward to shed rain. In the next course, use solid blocks over the vent.

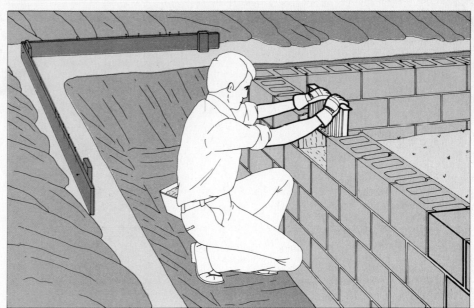

PARTITION BLOCK

4 **Making girder pockets.** In the final course, insert a partition block—a solid block 4 by 8 by 16 inches—at the center of each of the girder walls. Set the block flush with the outside, leaving a 4-inch-deep shelf inside for a pocket in which the girder will rest. Fill the cores of all exposed blocks with mortar, troweling flush with the tops. Build up the long walls, then proceed immediately to set anchor bolts (*Step 5*).

5 **Setting anchor bolts.** L-shaped anchor bolts, ½ inch thick and 8 inches long, are set into the mortar-filled cores a foot from each corner and every 4 feet in between. To set each bolt, place it in a jig—a 1-foot 2-by-6 with a ⅝-inch hole through the center—attach its washer and nut, and place the 2-by-6 flush with the outside of the block. Tap the anchor bolt into the wet mortar until the washer lies flat against the 2-by-6. After 24 hours, remove the nuts and washers and slide the 2-by-6s off the anchor bolts.

Supports for the Joists: Sills, Piers and Girder

1 Fastening the sill plate. Have a helper hold a section of sill plate—a perfectly straight 2-by-6 pressure-treated with preservative—on top of the final course of blocks with one end flush with the corner of the wall and with one side touching the anchor bolts. With a framing square, draw a line across the 2-by-6 at the center of each bolt; mark on each line the distance from the wall edge to the bolt center and drill a ¾-inch hole for each bolt. Fasten the sill plate over the bolts with their nuts and washers. Attach the remaining sections of sill plate and nail the ends together. Cut 5¾-by-4-inch notches in the girder-wall plates over each pocket.

2 Laying out the piers. Drive nails partway into the sill plates over the centers of the girder pockets and stretch a string between the nails. Have a helper measure off one third and two thirds of the distance between the outside edges of the foundation walls and mark the string with cloth strips at these points.

Using a plumb line, locate and dig holes for pier footings below the strips, excavating to the depth required by the local building code. Pour concrete footings and set precast concrete piers or build masonry-block piers (page 21) level with the bottoms of the girder pockets.

3 Making and setting the girder. Cut three 2-by-8s 1 inch shorter than the span between the backs of the girder pockets and fasten them together with staggered 16-penny nails every 10 inches. With one helper for every 5 feet of girder length, set this girder in the girder pockets, leaving ½ inch of air space between the ends of the girder and the backs of the pockets. Use steel plates or slate shims under the girder at the pockets and the piers to bring the top of the girder flush with the top of the sill plate. Cut several bricks in half and brick in the sides of the girder pocket, using ⅜-inch mortar joints between bricks and leaving ½ inch of air space on each side of the girder.

If the span of the girder is longer than 16 feet, splice separate lengths of 2-by-8. Stagger the splices and locate them directly above piers.

Constructing the Floor

1 **Marking the sill plates for joists.** Hook a tape measure—one long enough to stretch the length of the wall—to a nail driven 15½ inches from the end of a long wall and have a helper pull the tape taut. Set the tongue of a framing square (the leg that is 1½ inches wide) across the plate at 16-inch intervals, and draw lines on each side of the tongue. Mark the opposite plate in the same way, starting at the same end of the building. To mark the joist locations on the girder, stretch a chalk line between pairs of marks on the two walls and snap the line over the girder.

2 **Nailing header and stringer joists.** Set a long, straight 2-by-10 on edge as a header joist—placing it flush with the outside of the wall and parallel to the girder, and toenail it to the plate. Have a helper butt another 2-by-10 (a stringer joist) against the first at the corner, and nail the two boards together. Nail header and stringer joists for the other two sides of the foundation wall in the same way, toenailing them to the sill plate and to each other and butt-nailing them together at the corners.

With a framing square, extend the lines that you marked for floor joists in Step 1 onto the inside faces of the header joists.

3 **Nailing the regular joists.** Cut regular joists to fit between the header joists and the center of the girder. Set two regular joists in place between the header joists, lining them up with the marks on the insides of the headers; drive three 16-penny nails through the headers into the regular joists. Where the two regular joists meet, over the girder, toenail them to the girder, then sandwich them between two 9¼-inch squares of ⅜-inch plywood, nailed onto each side. Add a second pair of regular joists in the same way.

4 **Laying a vapor barrier.** Unroll a length of 3-foot-wide polyethylene sheeting over the crawl-space floor, beneath the two pairs of joists; cut off the sheeting, and weight the corners with rocks. Then nail in two more regular joists and unroll another length of sheeting, overlapping the first by 6 inches; again weight it with stones. Continue nailing joists, two at a time, and spreading polyethylene sheeting until you reach the far end of the foundation.

5 **Laying the subfloor.** Add blocking between joists at 4-foot intervals to stabilize the joists and provide nailing surfaces for plywood panels; toenail and face nail the blocking to the joists. Then lay ¾-inch exterior-grade plywood across the joists, and nail it down with eightpenny nails; space the nails 6 inches apart across the ends of the panels and 10 inches apart between ends. Stagger the end joints of the plywood panels, and leave gaps between the panels, ⅛ inch at the ends and 1⁄16 inch along the sides.

BLOCKING

Where to Find Land

When America's pioneers picked a spot for a cabin, they simply staked out a land claim in the wilderness, sharpened their axes and went to work. Putting up a cabin or cottage is more complex these days—and so is the job of locating a suitable building site. But finding land is still a necessary first step for a would-be cabin dweller: to move a project from the dream stage to the drawing board, you must have your site picked out or purchased.

Obviously, land is generally cheaper and more readily available in regions far from major metropolitan centers. But even in isolated areas, land prices are rising along with demand. Americans are competing for rural property—particularly for land near national or state parks, forests and recreation areas—and landowners and real estate agents are well aware that this is so. Yet a potential land-buyer need not resign himself to paying an outrageous price for property. There are still ways to find reasonably priced building sites, often without giving up easy access to recreational areas.

One prime source of vacation land in the United States is a group of some 200 government projects west of the Mississippi. Initiated by the U.S. Bureau of Reclamation, these projects generally begin with the damming of a river, creating reservoirs with thousands of miles of new shoreline. Most of these areas are supervised by the state agencies that cooperated in their original planning and construction.

At some of these projects cabinbuilders can lease small lots—the typical size is a quarter acre. Leasing conditions and restrictions vary widely from project to project and are subject to change, but when lots are available they can be had for astonishingly low prices; in one recent year, for example, lots were available at the Cedar Bluff and Lovewell Reservoirs in Kansas at annual rents of less than $50 for a 25-year term. For the latest information on the availability of such sites, apply to the appropriate state park or recreation department, or to the administrator of a specific project.

Canadians can lease or buy recreational building lots on publicly owned Crown lands. In recent years, for example, Ontario has made annual offerings, in approved subdivisions, of hundreds of lots ranging from three quarters to one acre. These properties are always advertised in the press, and are later parceled out to potential buyers or renters in a public drawing.

If you cannot lease or buy government land in the region you have picked for your retreat, you must turn to the private market. For the quickest information on where land is available—and at what price—start with the most obvious sources: classified advertising listings in a metropolitan newspaper in your chosen area, and the national or regional real estate companies that publish periodic catalogues of country properties. But remember that sellers of the remote parcels you are looking for do not advertise widely. In general, only properties near recreational areas or major highways turn up in the classified pages of major newspapers or the catalogues of agents—and such land is nearly always the most expensive.

Once you have settled on a specific area, look for local sources of information about land for sale. Subscribe to a leading small-town newspaper in the locale you have chosen. These papers frequently carry land-for-sale advertisements that do not appear in big-city newspapers or comprehensive catalogues. They are also good sources of local political and economic news that might affect land prices or influence your decision to buy. Plans for a major new recreational area, for example, would increase the cost of property.

Another place to learn of land that may be up for sale is the tax assessor's office in the county you are considering. Tax records are open to the public, and if you can locate a parcel with a heavy bill for back taxes, you might find that the owner would be willing to sell at a reasonable figure.

No matter where you decide to buy your land, there is no substitute for firsthand inspection, and regular visits to the area you have chosen can often turn up a desirable building site. Whenever you are in the area, talk to country storekeepers and service-station operators—they often can tell you of nearby landowners who might have property on the market.

You may, of course, decide that you want to build your cabin on private land near a national or state park or recreation area, even though land costs are likely to be higher than they would be for more remote sites. If so, building sites can frequently be found either within or adjacent to such lands, and you may be able to take advantage of a situation in which private land is partly administered or protected by the government. In New York State, for example, two huge preserves supervised by the state have been set aside in the Adirondack and Catskill Mountains, and there is a good deal of privately owned land available within these areas.

2

Four Simple Structures

A beam-and-pole sandwich. Pairs of beams, bolted to high poles, support the floor and roof of a pole-frame cabin *(pages 64-65)*. To make the beams lie flat and firm against the poles, shallow notches called daps are cut with a bucksaw on the sides of each pole; the beams are secured in the daps with threaded rods and nuts.

The choice of a foundation from among the possibilities described in Chapter 1 is generally based on such purely objective considerations as the requirements of a building code, or the lay of the land, or the depth of the frost line. Choosing a cabin to build on the foundation is a more personal matter. Esthetic preferences and personal life styles enter into the decision, and your first thoughts may be flights of fancy—perhaps a sophisticated chalet with an expanse of picture-window glass, or a forest retreat with a deck cantilevered over a lake. In the end, however, you are likely to turn to one of the four cabin types shown on the following pages. All can be built by an amateur with a minimum of special skills and tools. Each will suit a particular taste or solve a special construction problem.

The most common vacation cabin—and in fact the most common residential style in North America—is a frame structure with a skeleton of conventional stud walls. The design on pages 36-43 is especially adapted to the needs of a builder who lives so far from his building site that regular evening or weekend work on the site is impractical. Working at his own pace, whenever time is available, he assembles framing modules at home and sheathes them in plywood, with precut openings for doors and windows. The completed modules are trucked to the site and fitted together in a single day.

For a builder working on the site, the easiest cabin to assemble is the A-frame. Instead of framing a set of walls, putting in floor joists, then topping the structure with a roof, the builder assembles a set of huge triangles that combine the framing for walls, roof and floor in one. The triangles can be built on the ground with a minimum of joinery, then tilted into place. A single sheath serves as both roofing and siding, and the completed A-frame is at home anywhere: its steep pitch sheds snow in ski country, and its rigidity makes it stand up to wind and shifting sands at a beach site.

While an A-frame has a certain stark modernity of style, a log cabin harks back to America's pioneer past. To some people, a cabin made of anything but logs is not really a cabin at all, and few rustic buildings look more at home in their settings than a house of logs surrounded by trees. Like an A-frame, a log cabin requires no complicated framing: the logs are simply notched to fit together, then spiked between log courses for strength and stability.

Almost equally picturesque is the pole-frame cabin, in which long poles serve as both foundation and supporting members for the roof, and the building seems to nestle in a man-made cradle of tall timbers. This post-and-beam cabin is easy to build and has features of special usefulness; for example, no structure is better suited to an uneven terrain or to areas where flooding is a problem.

A Frame Cottage Built with Prefabricated Panels

The vacation house most like a year-round home has standard stud walls. Its great advantage for the amateur cabin builder is that it can be prefabricated in sections, hauled to the vacation site in a small truck and, with three or four helpers, quickly assembled on a prepared deck and topped with a simple rafter or truss roof *(pages 67-71 and 72-73)*. Using this method, you can erect the walls and roof of a cabin in a weekend.

The prefabricated parts are wall frames 7 feet 9 inches high and 4 feet, 8 feet, or 7 feet 8½ inches wide; these frames are made up of 2-by-4 studs and plates, and sheathed with ¾-inch plywood. Sections go together side by side to make walls of any size that is a multiple of 4 feet, a module suiting common building materials. Corner sections have projecting edges of sheathing that overlap to add strength. Jigs make possible fast and easy assembly of accurately sized sections.

You need plans that indicate the exact size of your foundation walls—so the panels will fit together properly—and also show the locations of doors, windows and intersecting walls. You may be able to simplify the job by ordering the doors and windows sized to fit exactly in the space occupied by studs. When transporting the panels, place them on a truck so that the last panel loaded is the first panel to be erected. Then you can simply back the truck up to the foundation and erect the panels on the deck.

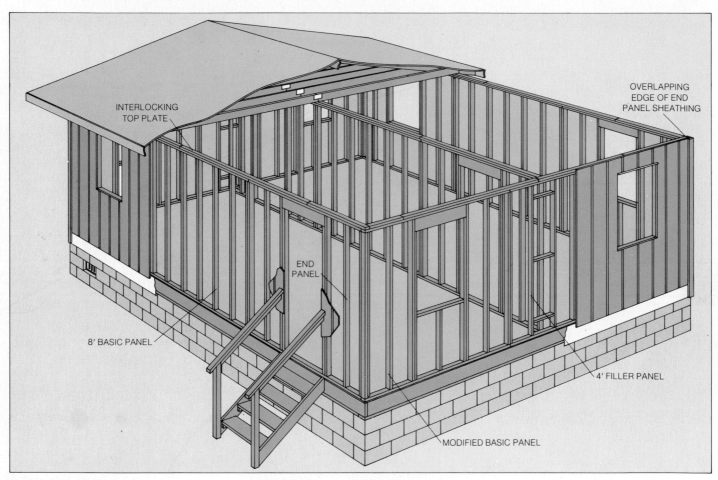

INTERLOCKING TOP PLATE

OVERLAPPING EDGE OF END PANEL SHEATHING

END PANEL

8' BASIC PANEL

4' FILLER PANEL

MODIFIED BASIC PANEL

Anatomy of a prefab. This example demonstrates how 12 prefabricated panels in three sizes make up the outer walls of a 20-by-24-foot cottage—any dimensions are attainable by varying the number of panels. One size panel serves as the basic module; another is a filler; the third serves for ends. At each corner, the basic panel is modified to provide a nailing surface for a projecting edge of sheathing on the adjoining end panel. Panels are nailed together where they abut, and firmly interconnected by an additional, overlapping top plate. For clarity, sheathing is not shown on some panels, but all actually are sheathed in advance.

Interior partitions are made up of the same kind of panels used for the exterior walls. The bearing partition rests on a girder running the length of the cottage. The studs at the sides of the windows illustrated are exactly 32 inches apart—the space of three studs. Any roof *(pages 67-73)* and foundation *(pages 14-31)* can be used.

The basic panel. Middle-of-the-wall sections are prefabricated of seven 2-by-4 studs, each 7 feet 4½ inches long, butt-nailed on 16-inch centers between 2-by-4 top and bottom plates, each 8 feet long. The sheathing, ¾-inch exterior-grade plywood, is nailed flush at the sides; it overlaps 1½ inches at the top to cover a second top plate, and 3 inches at the bottom so that rain drips off. The second top plate is added after the panels are erected. A basic panel 4 feet wide but otherwise identical serves as a filler so walls can be made in multiples of 4 feet. Windows and doors can be installed in the panels as indicated in the drawings at right below.

The modified basic panel. To tie the walls together at the corners, the basic panel is modified by adding an extra stud butted to the corner stud. The extra nailer stud serves as a surface for attaching the corner panel (*bottom*) as well as interior wallboard.

The drawing also illustrates the additional changes required in any panel to assemble a rough frame for a window: a header, made by nailing together two 2-by-6s with a ½-inch plywood spacer; jack studs to support the header; a rough sill toenailed to the jack studs; and a cripple stud under the rough sill.

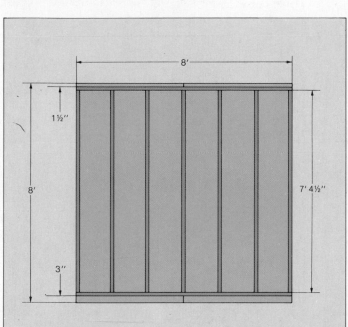

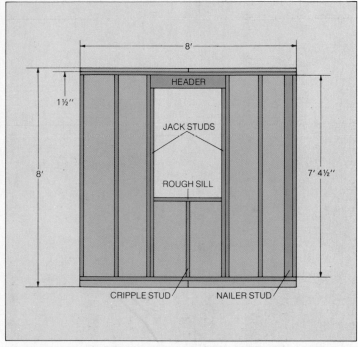

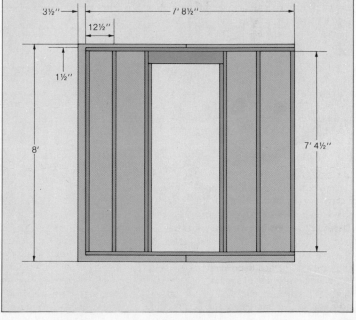

The corner panel. The frame of this panel is only 7 feet 8½ inches long and is covered by sheathing that overlaps the corner end by 3½ inches. The overlapped portion of the sheathing is nailed to the end stud of the modified basic panel (*top, right*). Because the sheathing always overlaps to the right when viewed from outside, the walls must be erected from left to right. This drawing illustrates the modifications that must be made in any panel for a door: a header and jack studs like those shown above for a window in a modified basic panel.

Walls from an Assembly Line

SAW GUIDE

SIDE STOP

END STOP

1 **Mass-producing studs.** Using a power saw and a jig, cut all studs for each panel at once—you need seven studs for each full-sized section without openings, plus an extra for each modified basic panel. Make the jig from a securely mounted plywood sheet. Nail an 8-foot 2-by-4 stop along one side and a 2-by-2 stop at right angles to it. At the opposite end of the side stop, hinge a 2-by-2 saw guide so that it can be lifted to slide the stud lumber underneath it.

Position the guide at right angles to the side stop so that, when the saw shoe is touching it, the saw blade will be 7 feet 4½ inches from the end stop. Check angles and distances at several points to be sure the guide is parallel to the end stop and a proper distance from it.

2 **Framing panels.** For the basic panel without doors or windows, butt-nail studs on 16-inch centers between 8-foot or 4-foot top and bottom plates. Make as many basic panels as the size of your cottage requires. Make four modified basic panels the same way except at the corners, where they adjoin end panels; there a stud assembly is built up from two 2-by-4s, the edge of one butted against the face of the other (*inset*) to provide a projecting nailing surface.

For the end panels, butt-nail studs between plates 7 feet 8½ inches long, using 16-inch spacing for all studs except the one that will be at the corner; it is spaced 12½ inches from its neighbor. Number each panel to match your plan.

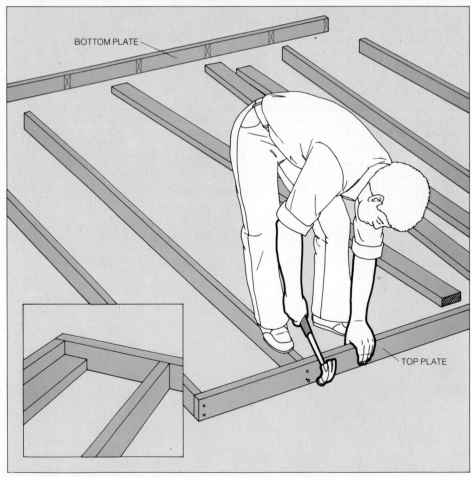

BOTTOM PLATE

TOP PLATE

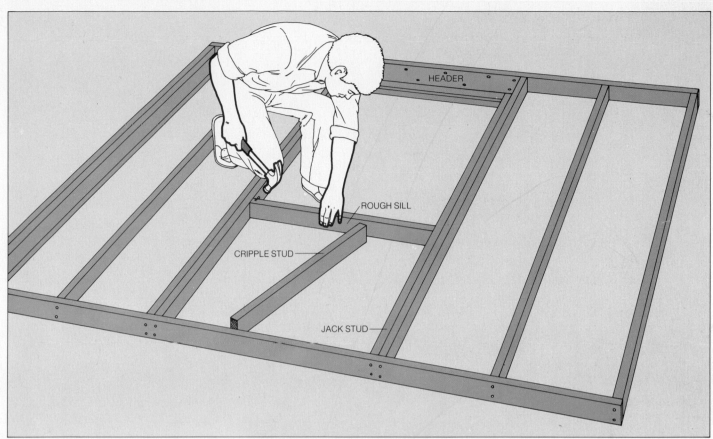

HEADER

ROUGH SILL

CRIPPLE STUD

JACK STUD

3 **Framing rough openings.** For a window that requires a rough opening 30½ inches wide, omit one stud, set the centers of the adjoining studs 35 inches apart and toenail across the top of the opening a header—two 2-by-6s, 33½ inches long with a ½-inch plywood spacer between; beneath the header, nail jack studs to the studs that flank the header, making each jack stud 6 feet 11 inches long. To the jack studs toenail a 2-by-4 rough sill, carefully leveled, at the height specified by the manufacturer of your window. Butt-nail a 2-by-4 cripple stud cut to fit between the rough sill and the bottom plate. For a door with the same rough opening, install a header and jack studs as for a window.

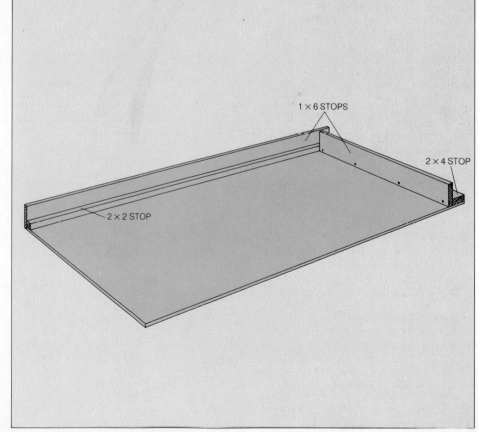

1 × 6 STOPS

2 × 4 STOP

2 × 2 STOP

4 **A jig for sheathing.** To a 4-by-8 sheet of plywood, nail a 2-by-2 stop 8 feet long along one end and a 2-by-4 stop 3 feet 10½ inches long along one side. Nail a 1-by-6 to the inside of the 2-by-4 and another to the outside of the 2-by-2.

5 **Sheathing basic panels.** Slide each basic and modified basic panel into the jig, placing its end against the short stop and its top plate against the long stop, slide a sheet of ¾-inch exterior-grade plywood against the 1-by-6 stops and nail to the frame beneath with galvanized six-penny nails every 6 inches at the edges and every 12 inches at intermediate studs. Slide a second sheet of sheathing plywood into place, with its side against the first sheet and its top against the long stop, and nail it as you did the first sheet.

To cut the door and window openings, drill pilot holes through the interior side of the sheathing at the top and bottom of each rough frame, use a straightedge to connect the holes on the exterior side and saw out the outlined opening.

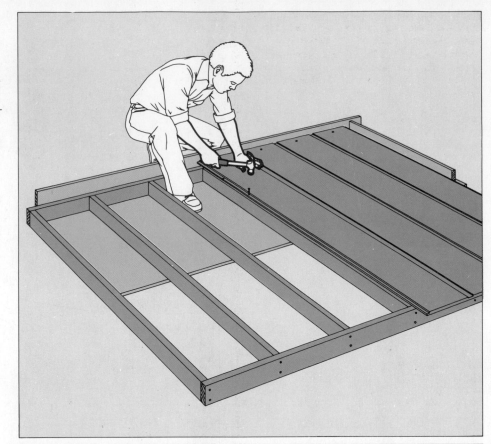

6 **Sheathing end panels.** Modify the sheathing jig by moving the 1-by-6 attached to the 2-by-4 stop from the inside to the outside (*inset*), then slide end frames and sheathing into the jig and nail them, using the method of Step 5.

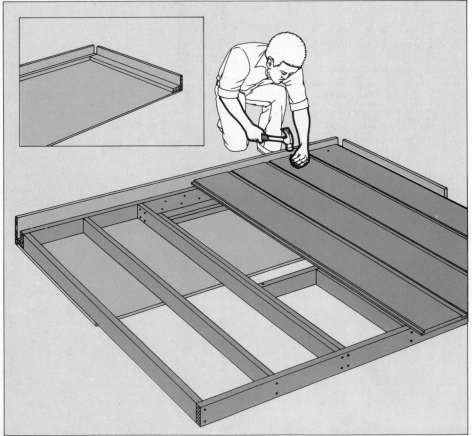

7 **Flashing the openings.** With metal shears, cut pieces of 6-inch aluminum flashing the width of each rough opening. Use a cold chisel or pry bar to loosen the sheathing around the header; then, wearing gloves, slip the flashing between the header and the sheathing, and hammer the sheathing down tight again.

Erecting the Walls

1 **Bracing the first panel.** After building a foundation and installing joists *(pages 26-31)*, tilt a modified basic panel into position at a corner, fasten the bottom plate to the subfloor and brace it with a diagonal 2-by-4 eight feet long tacked in place. After a helper plumbs the panel, nail the brace in place and add a second brace at the other end of the panel.

2 **Extending the wall.** While a helper holds the next panel in position, use a 4-pound sledge to drive the panel into alignment with the adjoining panel. If the deck is warped, drive the bottom plate of the new panel down until the end studs of both panels are flush. Secure, brace and plumb the new panel *(page 41, Step 1)*.

Erect three walls using modified basic panels at the right of each corner (as seen from outside the cottage) and end panels to complete the corners. Bring in the interior partitions and put up the fourth wall. Drive sixpenny nails through the overlapping sheathing on end panels and into the corner studs of the modified basic panels.

3 **Tying the walls together.** Nail a 2-by-4 plate 4 feet long to the top plate of an end panel so that it overlaps the top plate of a modified basic panel. Install additional 8-foot plates, lapping the joints between the remaining panels; cut the last plate in a wall flush with the wall end, and finish with a 4-foot plate if necessary. If a panel is bowed, have a helper push it in or out until the top plates align, before you nail them together.

Slip strips of aluminum flashing under the sheathing, overlapping the foundation wall by 3 inches, and drive sixpenny galvanized nails through the flashing and into header joists every 6 inches. Cover the edges of the sheathing at corners with butted 1-by-3s and 1-by-4s.

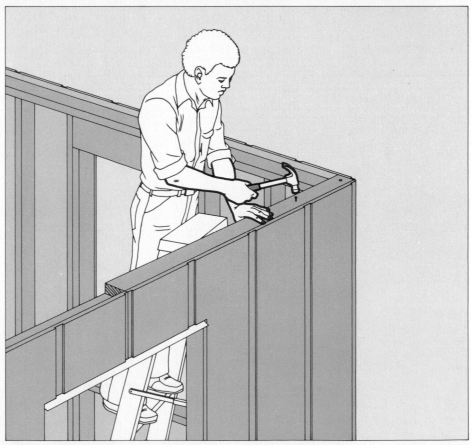

4 **Marking for the interior wall.** Snap two parallel chalk lines 3½ inches apart on the subfloor between the side walls. Use the girder pockets (*page 29, Step 4*) as reference points to center the lines directly over the girder.

3½″

5 **Setting the interior partitions.** Nail 2-by-4 blocks between side-wall studs above the chalk lines made in Step 4. Fasten the blocks near the top, center and bottom of the studs. (If you plan to install wallboard inside the side walls, do it at this point.) Erect and brace the interior partitions directly over the chalk lines (*Steps 1 and 2*), nailing the end panels to the blocks. Tie the partitions together (*Step 3*).

2 × 4 BLOCK

The A-Frame: A String of Sturdy Triangles

An A-frame is one of the simplest and sturdiest of all structures. Its skeleton is a row of triangles—the bases of the triangles are the joists that support the floor and the sides of the triangles are the rafters that hold the combined walls and roof. With sheathing in place on top of the skeleton, this elementary structure is one of the strongest known.

The A-frame's simplicity of construction and comparatively low cost make it a popular choice for vacation cabins. The slope and strength of its roof are particularly well suited to snow country, but an A-frame can make a comfortable vacation home anywhere, from the mountains to the beach. Its high, peaked ceiling gives a spacious feeling to the smallest cabin. The inward-sloping walls create low, awkward areas on both sides of the house, but these spaces can be turned into convenient storage places.

An A-frame can be built to almost any size simply by varying the dimensions and number of the triangles in its skeleton, but a cabin with a sleeping loft must be built of triangles measuring at least 17 feet on a side, to allow adequate headroom above both floors. Keep in mind also that at board lengths greater than 20 feet, lumber costs increase radically and availability may be limited, and that triangles more than 24 feet on a side may be too unwieldy for a crew of amateurs.

The shape of the triangles can vary from gently to steeply sloped, but the most common shape is equilateral, with joists and rafters of equal lengths and angles of 60°. This shape simplifies ordering and cutting the lumber for the skeleton and gives adequate headroom for a minimum amount of lumber. If you choose to build an A-frame that is not equilateral, you must use a scale drawing or trigonometry to determine the lengths of the rafters and the angles of the cuts.

An A-frame's triangles are bolted and nailed together on the ground, then lifted into place atop continuous masonry-block foundation walls (pages 26-31) or a foundation of poles (or piers) and girders (pages 14-21) like the one shown below. For a small A-frame (up to 24 feet), the lifting can be done by three people with no special equipment. When the triangles are up and sheathed, the floor is laid

and interior partitions can be erected in any arrangement.

A sleeping loft must be provided with stairs or a ladder (the choice depending on the amount of available space on the first floor) and a sturdy railing. Doors and windows are framed in the end walls with 2-by-4 studs—large A-frames require a lot of window space if they are not to be dark in the middle. A deck, if you build one, should be surrounded by a sturdy railing and should rest on the same foundation as the main structure. Stairs to the deck can be ordered from a stair-builder or constructed on the job with 2-by-10 stringers and 2-by-10 treads.

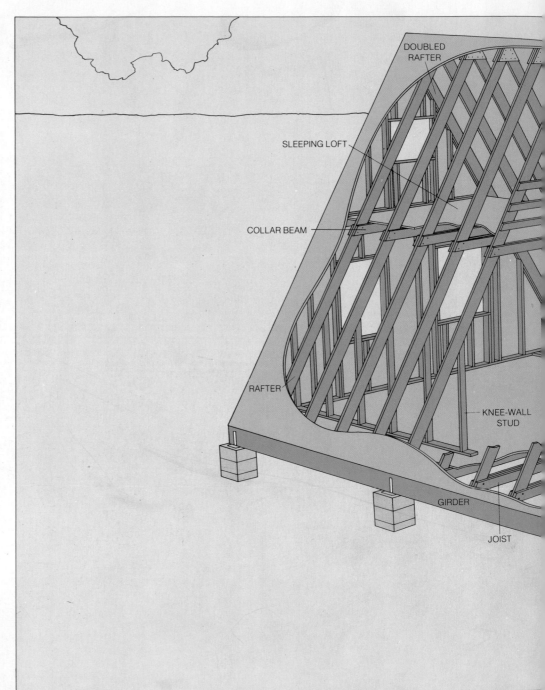

A basic A-frame cabin. This small equilateral A-frame rests on a foundation of tripled 2-by-10 girders supported by concrete-block piers. The triangles of the skeleton, spaced 24 inches apart on center, are formed of 2-by-8 rafters joined at the apexes with plywood gussets and sandwiched at the bottom corners by pairs of 2-by-6 joists. (Triangles spaced wider apart would require heavier rafters and joists.) At the end walls and under the sleeping loft, horizontal 2-by-6 collar beams sandwich the rafters like extra joists. The rafters of the end walls are doubled in order to provide a flush nailing surface for the exterior sheathing.

The sleeping loft, reached by a ladder, sits over the rear of the cabin. Knee walls along the sides of the cabin square off the low corners where the rafters meet the floor, and conceal a convenient storage space. The deck rests on 2-by-6 joists set 16 inches apart on center. Posts for the railing are secured to the deck joists; the stairs are set on concrete footings and are attached to the deck with metal fasteners.

GUSSET

JOIST

PIER

Putting Up the Frame

1 Cutting joists and rafters. After building a foundation and installing girders, make a jig to cut the joists by nailing to a work surface two 2-by-4s 5½ inches apart and nailing across them a 1-by-2 at the angle of the joist ends—for the equilateral A-frame illustrated, 60°. Run a circular saw along the guide, cutting a kerf into both 2-by-4s.

Mark each 2-by-6 joist for length—the width of the cabin—slip it into the jig so that the end mark is at the kerf in the jig and cut the joist.

Cut both ends to angle toward the middle. Make a similar jig to fit rafters, spacing the 2-by-4s 7½ inches, and add an adjustable guide. Cut the rafters with one end at the same angle as the joists and the other at the angle of the peak cut (for an equilateral A-frame, 60° and 30° respectively). Determine the rafter length from the width of the cabin and the slope of its roof, using an accurate scale drawing or trigonometry (for the equilateral A-frame, the rafters are the same length as the joists).

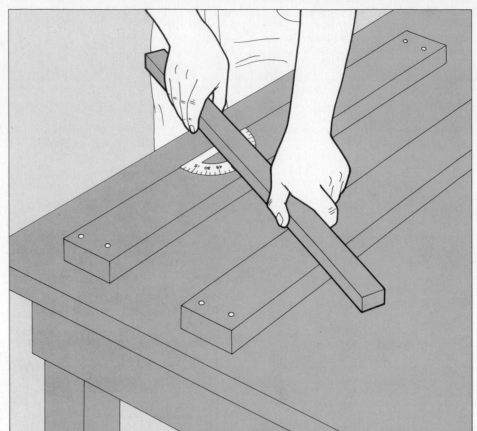

2 Assembling the triangles. Clamp the ends of two joists around the base of a rafter, align the edges so that the boards meet at the correct angle, and drill through the three boards. Fasten them with a ⅝-inch carriage bolt. Bolt the other ends of the joists to the base of another rafter and complete the triangle by joining the rafter peaks with two gussets of ¾-inch exterior-grade plywood nailed to the rafters (*inset*). Then add a second carriage bolt to the joint at the base of each rafter. Assemble all the triangles in the same manner, but on each of the end triangles nail a gusset to just one face of the rafters.

On one of the assembled triangles, mark the top edge of each rafter at the height at which you wish to attach collar beams, allowing for sufficient headroom—at least 7 feet. In the jig you used for the joists (*Step 1*), cut collar beams to the distance between the two rafter marks and bolt them on as you did the joists. Slip short 2-by-4 spacer blocks between all the pairs of joists and collar beams at 2-foot intervals and nail the blocks in place.

Using the rafter jig, cut 2-by-8 boards to fit flush against the outside faces of the end rafters, one set of boards between the joists and the collar beams and another from the collar beams to the peaks; nail the boards in place.

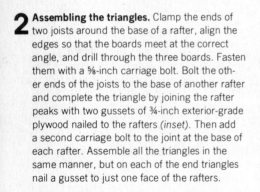

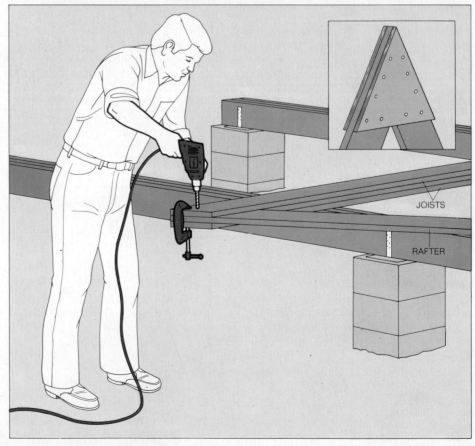

JOISTS

RAFTER

3 **Erecting the triangles.** You will need two help- ers to lift the triangles into position and to steady and plumb them as you attach braces to the rafters. Mark the girders for the triangles on 2-foot centers, then nail scabs—1- to 2-foot 2-by-4s—to the insides of the outer girders next to the marks for the front end triangle. Set the base of the end triangle against the scabs, raise the triangle plumb and brace it with 2-by-4s run diagonally from the rafters to the girders.

Raise and plumb the remaining triangles as you did the first, bracing each with a pair of hori- zontal braces nailed across the rafters on both sides of the erect triangles. Set the braces at least 4½ feet from the base of the rafters.

As each triangle is erected and secured with hori- zontal braces, anchor its bottom corners to the girders with metal anchor plates on both sides of the joists and nail through the corners of the rafters and joists into the girders. Sheathe the skeleton with 4-by-8 panels of ¾-inch exterior- grade plywood, removing the temporary braces after the bottom course of panels is in place. Cover the main floor and the floor of the sleeping loft, if you have one, with similar 4-by-8 panels.

Filling In the Walls

1 **Marking the plates.** Cut top and sole plates to fit from rafter to rafter along the floor and the un- derside of the collar beam; nail down the sole plate along the outer edge of the floor and center the top plate next to it. Mark the plates for studs spaced 16 inches on center, leaving space between two stud marks for a door.

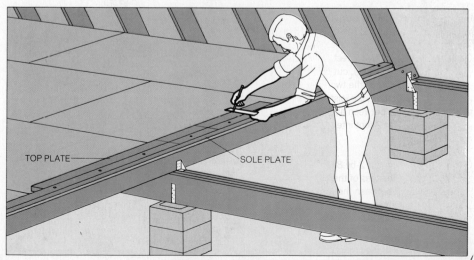

2 **Assembling the end wall.** Cut studs to fit between the top and sole plates; cut headers and jack and cripple studs to frame a door and window. Butt-nail the studs to the top plate at the marked locations and complete the door and window framing. With a helper, lift the stud assembly into place and align the top plate flush with the outer edge of the outer collar beam. Nail the top plate to the underside of the collar beam, then plumb the studs and toenail them to the sole plate at the marks made in Step 1.

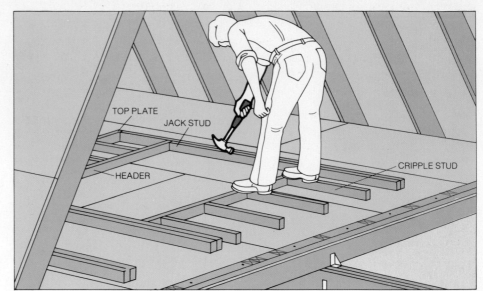

TOP PLATE

JACK STUD

HEADER

CRIPPLE STUD

3 **Marking beveled studs.** Stand a 2-by-4 on a piece of 2-by-4 next to each remaining marked location on the sole plate; plumb the 2-by-4 and mark a line along its edge where it meets the bottom edge of the rafter. Cut the 2-by-4 along the line and toenail it to the doubled end rafters and to the sole plate.

Frame the rest of the wall below and above the collar beams and frame the other end wall in the same manner. Sheathe both walls with ¾-inch exterior plywood, staggering joints.

Putting In a Knee Wall

Framing the knee wall. To close off the low corners where the sloping roof meets the floor at the sides of the house, build knee walls from the floor to the rafters. To make a knee wall, cut a 2-by-4 sole plate the length of the wall and mark its ends on the floor directly under two rafters. Mark the plate for studs to extend to each rafter above it. Stand a 2-by-4 on the plate next to one of the marks and mark the 2-by-4 as you did the stud in Step 3 (*opposite*). Cut the 2-by-4 at the mark and use it as a template to mark and cut the remaining studs.

Butt-nail the cut studs to the sole plate, tilt the assembly into position, and nail the plate to the floor and the studs to the rafters. If the knee wall does not extend to the end of the house, run a second sole plate from the first across to the rafter, and cover the open end with wallboard.

Partition walls that fit between the floor and the collar beams are framed like end walls.

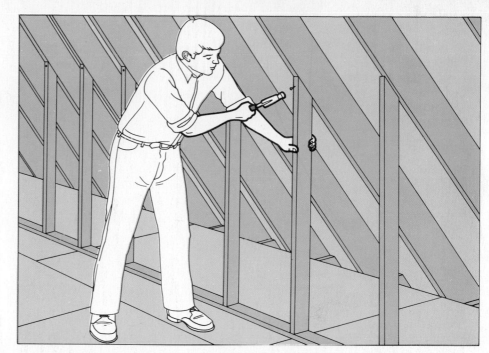

Finishing the Loft

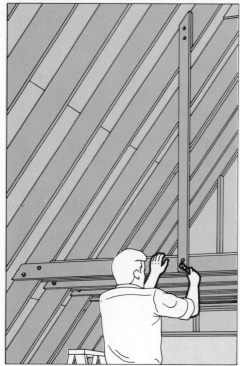

1 Securing posts for a rail. After installing a loft floor, mark locations a ladder-width apart for two 2-by-4 posts on the front collar beam; with a helper, cut the 2-by-4s to fit from the bottom of the beam to the top of the rafters; attach the bottom of each to the collar beam with a lag bolt. Plumb the posts and bolt them to the rafters with two ½-inch carriage bolts, using 2-by-4 blocking between posts and rafters. Add a second lag bolt to the bottom of each post.

2 Attaching the rails. Cut 2-by-4 top rails to overlap the posts and the rafters 3 feet above the floor of the loft. Bolt each rail to the rear face of the post and to the front face of the rafter with two ½-inch carriage bolts. Add lower rails spaced no more than 6 inches apart. Build your own ladder or buy a simple wooden one at a

hardware store and attach it to the collar beam with metal anchor plates.

If you want stairs rather than a ladder, you can conserve space by installing fold-up attic stairs, available in kits, in a trap-door-covered hole in the floor. Set the stairs parallel to the rafters.

Building a Deck

1 **Laying the understructure.** Fasten 20-foot 2-by-6 deck joists as long as the cabin width to the cabin girders with metal anchors 16 inches apart (*page 47, Step 3*), placing one end joist flush against the outer joist of the first triangle (notch the deck joist to fit over projecting nuts or bolt heads). Butt-nail 2-by-6 perimeter boards to the deck-joist ends at each side.

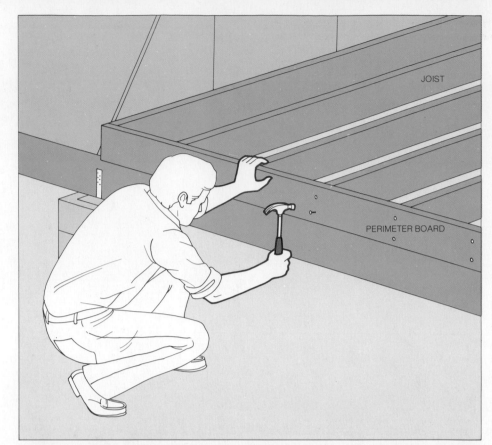

2 **Installing posts for railings.** At each corner of the deck, set a 4-by-4 post 4 feet long on the girder, and bolt the post to the end joist with two carriage bolts and to the perimeter board with a third. Bolt a similar post inside the outer joist at either side of the stairway opening with three carriage bolts, resting one post on the center girder if possible, and bracing both by bolting them to pieces of 2-by-6 blocking nailed between joists.

For decking, nail 2-by-6s across the joists, spacing the boards ¼ inch apart.

3 **Completing the rail.** Screw 2-by-4 rails to the outside faces of the posts, working up from the lower rails and spacing them no more than 6 inches apart. To enclose the small triangular space next to the end wall of the house, run rails from the nearby corner post on each side to a stud in the end wall. Screw the rails to the corner post, nail them to the stud, and on each side toenail an additional 4-by-4 post to the ends of the rails and the top of the deck.

Set 2-by-4 top rails on top of the posts; miter them at the corners for a neat fit.

4 **Mounting the stairway.** Pour concrete footings for the stairway stringers and fasten the tops of the stringers to the outer deck joist with metal anchors. Bolt 4-by-4 bottom posts for the handrails to the outside faces of the stringers and nail 2-by-4 handrails to the bottom posts and to the stairway posts on the deck, keeping the rails parallel with the stairway stringers.

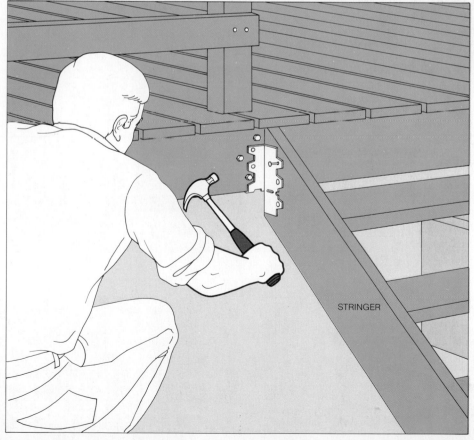

STRINGER

From the Frontier, a Cabin of Hand-hewn Logs

The elaborate framing and sheathing techniques required in most types of construction are not needed to build a log cabin. Instead, logs are notched to fit over each other to form interlocking walls, out of which openings for doors and windows are later cut. The techniques used today are almost identical to those employed by the pioneer settlers 200 years ago, the major modernization being the substitution of a chain saw for an ax as chief tool.

Dozens of precut log-home kits are sold in a variety of designs, but if you can procure and prepare your own logs, you can build a log cabin at far less cost. The trees best suited to log construction are softwoods—cedar, pine, fir and larch—that measure 8 to 12 inches in diameter and taper very little from butt to tip. To calculate the number of logs you will need, add the heights in inches of all the walls in your plan—including gables at the end walls—and divide by the average diameter in inches of the logs you will

use. To this basic count, add a few extra logs to allow for mistakes. For your rafters (pages 60-61), get straight, smooth logs 5 to 6 inches thick.

Using the techniques shown on pages 10-12, you can fell logs on your own land; in some areas, you can log land of the National Forests or of a local lumber company by paying a "stumpage fee." Occasionally you can buy logs seasoned, peeled and ready for use from a local utility company or logging company.

Whenever possible, cut logs in late fall or early winter, while the sap is down. To prevent excessive cracking, use a spud (below) to peel a 2-inch strip from the two roughest opposite faces of each log before you stack them. These will be the top and bottom faces, and any cracking that occurs will be localized in these strips, which you will conceal as you build. Stack the partially peeled logs in one or two layers, spacing them about 3 inches apart to allow air to circulate between them, cover them with pine

boughs and turn them every month or so to prevent uneven bleaching and drying. When the logs have cured for at least six months, peel them and soak or paint them with a commercial preservative to repel insects and prevent decay.

The considerable weight of log walls requires a continuous foundation of stone or masonry block. You can build a log cabin on the foundation described on pages 26-31, modifying it to accommodate the offset levels of the logs by building up the end walls with an additional course of half blocks. Long anchor bolts, projecting 7½ inches above the foundation wall, are needed in the side walls, but bolts are not used in the end walls; the end logs are notched over bolted sill logs in the side walls. The sill logs are the keystone of the structure and must be squared off to fit snugly against the foundation and to accommodate joist hangers. Though you can square off your own sill logs with a chain saw, many builders use pressure-treated 8-by-8 timbers.

Time-honored Tools

The chain saw has replaced many of the unique tools once used in log construction but a few old devices, available from specialized tool or antique dealers, remain essential:

☐ THE CANT HOOK, a pole with a spiked hook at one end, makes it easy to move heavy logs short distances.

☐ THE PEELING SPUD, or SLICK, with its shovel-like blade, strips bark off logs.

☐ LOG DOGS are 3-foot iron bars with turned points at each end. The points are driven into a log and a nearby support to secure a log while you work on it. Get at least four of them for the job of building a log cabin.

☐ THE DRAWKNIFE is a long double-handled blade pulled toward the user to shave and smooth log surfaces.

If you cannot find log dogs, you can substitute 2-by-4s with a spike at each end; you can shorten and sharpen the blade of a shovel for a peeling spud.

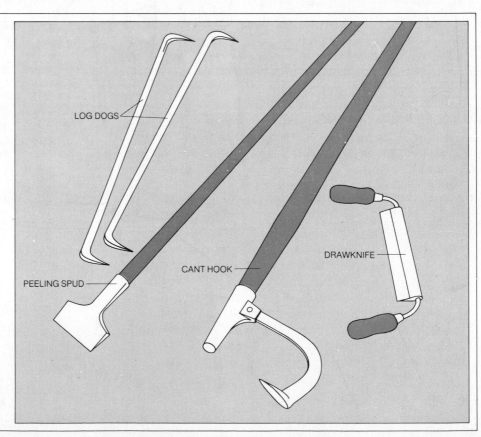

LOG DOGS

PEELING SPUD

CANT HOOK

DRAWKNIFE

Anatomy of a log cabin. The masonry foundation for this cabin is identical to the one on pages 26-31 except that the gable walls have an extra half course extending to within 8 inches of the corners. Joists, supported by joist hangers, run between 8-by-8 sills bolted to the side foundation walls. The bottom end logs are flattened to rest on the end foundation walls and notched at each end to fit over the sills.

Notched logs, laid alternately butt to tip, serve to build up the walls. Spikes, driven 2 feet from every corner and on both sides of door and window openings, secure each log to the one below it. (In this drawing only the spikes at the right corner are shown.)

At the tops of the front and back walls, plate logs with squared top and outside faces simplify

the notching of rafter logs, which are spiked together at the roof ridge. Snow-blocks cut from 2-by-4s fit between rafters to plug the air spaces above the plate logs and below the roof. Gable logs are spiked directly to one another.

For a log cabin with a shed roof, simply stack the end-wall logs with all the butts at the front or back of the cabin to build up a higher wall.

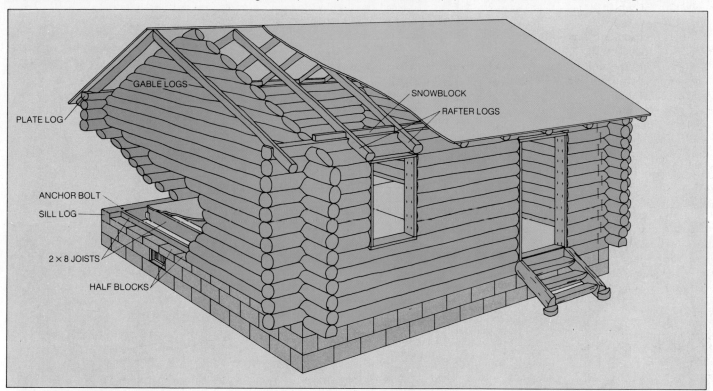

GABLE LOGS

PLATE LOG

SNOWBLOCK

RAFTER LOGS

ANCHOR BOLT

SILL LOG

2 × 8 JOISTS

HALF BLOCKS

Fitting the First Courses

1 Drilling the sill logs. After building a foundation and setting in anchor bolts *(page 29)*, transfer bolt locations from the foundation to the sill log *(page 30)*. Using a ½-inch drill fitted with a 1½-inch bit, drill a 2-inch hole at each bolt location; then, using a ¾-inch electrician's bit, extend each hole through the sill log.

Set the sills over the bolts and, starting 8 inches from the end of each sill, mark joist positions on 16-inch centers *(page 31, Step 1)*. Install joist hangers at the marks, nail joists to the hangers and lay a subfloor.

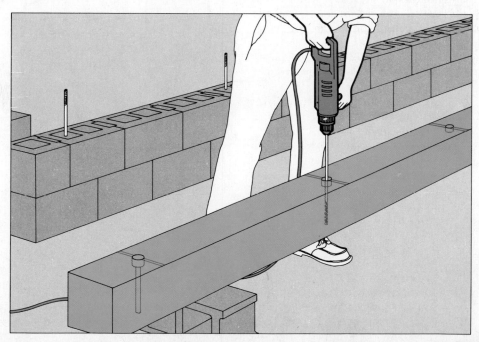

2 **Flattening the first two end logs.** Rest the first two end logs on a pair of timbers, butt their bottom faces—one of the sides peeled before drying to localize cracking—and secure them with log dogs. Then, starting at one end, run a chain saw between the logs, reposition them to close the gap you have created and repeat the process until you have made a flat surface—3 to 4 inches wide—on each log.

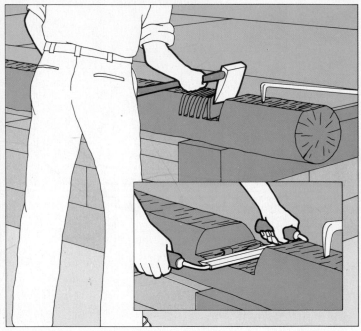

3 **Marking notches on the first end logs.** Position both gable-end logs over the sill logs, with equal lengths overhanging each corner, and check diagonals (page 26) to square them. Secure them with log dogs and, holding a carpenter's level against the outside face of an end log, mark the position of the sill log at two points 4 inches above the top of the sill. Connect the marks with a straightedge. Similarly mark the inside face of the end log. Repeat the process to mark the other corner and the other end log.

Remove the log dogs, roll each end log toward the interior of the cabin and secure it flat side up. Connect the marks at each log end, using an open section of stovepipe as a template (inset).

4 **Cutting the notches.** With the logs still secured, make vertical cuts to the marked depth with a chain saw and chop out waste wood with an ax. Finish the corners of the notch with a chisel and mallet, and smooth the bottom with a drawknife (inset).

After you have finished the notches, remove the log dogs and roll the logs into position over the sill logs. Mark any bumps that prevent the logs from sitting properly, secure the logs notch side up and trim them with a drawknife.

Spread oakum or caulking compound where the end logs will rest on the foundation and sill logs; roll the end logs into place.

How to Raise a Log Wall

Raising a log wall is largely a process of approximation and compensation, unlike the precise measuring and planning procedure involved in building with milled lumber. The logs go up building-block fashion, one at a time, and they are trued in the same piecemeal way. As each log is placed, it is checked with a level and plumb bob; if the wall begins to stray from level or plumb, the next logs are worried into positions that compensate for the drift.

Choosing like-sized logs for corresponding positions in opposite walls is the first way to keep the walls level. Use matched pairs of thick logs at the bottoms of opposite walls; pair off thinner logs near the tops. A second trick for keeping courses level is alternating the thick ends, or butts, of the logs in each wall to compensate for their taper.

Even the most careful log selection will not always produce a level, plumb wall; in some cases you must make adjustments by changing the size of the corner notch—the crucial cut in the bottom of each log that locks walls together at the corners. A notch that is shallower than others will make a log ride higher to lift the end of a wall that is beginning to dip; a deeper notch will lower the end. Be careful when making these adjustments: a log notched too deeply rests along its length on the log below, and a structurally unsound gap, called a mousehole, appears at the top of the notch. If you see that you have opened a mousehole, trim wood from the bottom of the notched log until the entire weight of the log hangs from the notches.

The depth of the corner notches also controls the size of the gaps between logs, and the depth of these notches is controlled in turn by the dividers used to mark them. Setting the dividers as shown at right will leave the smallest practical gap; if you want wider gaps, set the divider points in the same way, then slightly decrease the distance between them before marking the notch. Walls built with wide gaps require fewer logs and take less time to build, but they are poor insulators and the job of filling in the gaps, called chinking (page 63), is especially difficult. You must, in any case, observe certain limits in setting gaps and notches: never make a gap wider than 2 inches or a notch deeper than half the diameter of a log.

As a wall rises, a lifting aid is needed to wrestle the logs into place. The simplest consists of two leaning poles that form a ramp for rolling the logs up to the top of the wall. To avoid the hazards of cutting notches while standing on high scaffolding, some builders raise the wall to a low height, then move the highest logs to masonry blocks resting on the ground and build the top courses there. When these courses have been properly fitted, the builder numbers the logs, reassembles them in their correct positions on the top of the wall, and spikes them in place (page 56, Step 3).

Doors and windows for a log wall can be made from scratch or bought pre-hung. Their finish frames of jambs and sills or thresholds are placed in the standard way but a rough frame especially suited to log structures must be built for them (page 58, Step 4). These rough frames, made with an air space at the top and nailed in place through predrilled slots, allow the walls to settle gradually without racking the doors and windows.

Notching and Fitting Logs

1 **Scribing the notch.** Use log dogs to secure the first wall log across the end logs and directly over the sill, then lock the points of a pair of wing dividers to the distance between the wall log and the sill. Rest one point on the bottom of the wall log and the other against the side of the end log; then, keeping the points in a vertical line and in contact with both logs, move the dividers up and over the end log to scratch the end log's contours into the underside of the wall log. Repeat the operation on the opposite side of the wall log to complete the markings for the notch, then scribe the other end of the wall log in the same way.

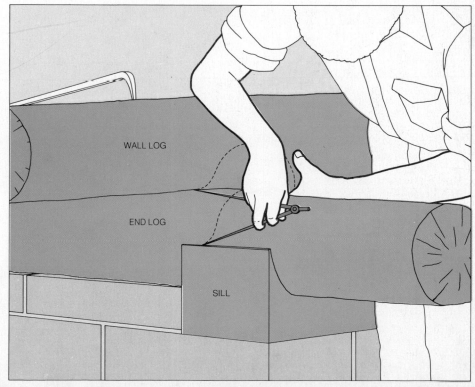

WALL LOG

END LOG

SILL

2 **Cutting a notch.** Secure the scribed log upside down, make several vertical cuts down each notch almost to the scribed lines with a chain saw (*below, left*) and cut out most of the waste wood with an ax or with a chisel and mallet. To trim the wood precisely to the scribed lines, use the chisel called a gouge; use a 2-inch gouge with an outside bevel (*below, right*). Cut the center of the notch about 1 inch deeper than the edges. Roll the log into place and mark any high spots that keep the notches from settling snugly onto the logs below. Roll the log upside down again and trim the high spots with a drawknife or a gouge.

As each pair of logs is fitted into place, measure to their tops from the subfloor at the corners of the cabin. If the measurements vary by more than an inch, level the next course by using logs with especially thick or thin ends, or by adjusting the depth of the notches. To be sure the walls are square, make regular checks of the diagonal measurements between corners —they should be identical.

3 **Spiking the logs.** Drive spikes to secure each course to the course below it. To prepare a course for spiking, drill ¾-inch holes halfway through the logs about 2 feet from each corner and about 1 foot from each side of a planned door or window opening. Extend the holes to the bottom of the course with a ⁷/₁₆-inch bit, then into each hole drive a spike ½ inch thick and long enough to reach the middle of the log below. Using a long machine bolt as a punch, drive the spikes well into the log beneath. Mark the spike locations and stagger the spikes in each new course.

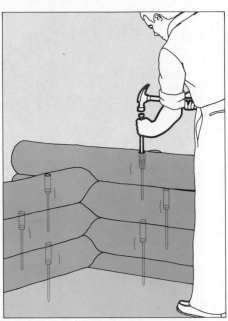

4 **Rolling logs up a wall.** When the wall gets too high for logs to be lifted into place easily, lean two sturdy poles against the wall at about a 45° angle and spike their ends to the projecting ends of the top logs of the adjacent walls. Tie ropes to the top log of the wall you are raising, loop the ropes down under the log to be hoisted and back to the top of the wall and, with a helper, pull the free ends of the ropes to roll the log up the poles.

When you have placed the highest log that will have to be cut out for a door or window opening, cut two V-shaped notches into its top just inside the edges of the planned opening (*inset*); make the notches deep enough to serve as starter holes for a chain saw.

5 **Squaring the plate logs.** To make square plate logs for the tops of the side walls, choose two logs with little or no taper and flatten their top faces *(page 54, Step 2)*; then secure the logs alongside each other with the flat faces upward and flatten the facing sides in the same way. Continue removing wood until the side and top faces form a true right angle. Finally, trim and smooth this corner with a drawknife.

Cutting and Framing for Doors and Windows

1 **Nailing up guide strips.** Nail vertical guide strips to the interior walls as far apart as the width of the door or window unit (including jambs) plus 4 inches; run the strips from the floor or below the window sill to points above the planned opening, and use a level to make sure that the boards are vertical. Fasten matching strips to the outsides of the walls, aligning them to the inner strips with a straightedge pushed through the gaps between logs. Inside the cabin, measure up from the subfloor a distance 5 inches greater than the height of the door unit and mark the top of the opening with a level. You can put a window at any convenient height as long as the bottom of the opening is not between logs. Mark the top and bottom of a window opening with horizontal lines as far apart as the height of the window unit plus 6 inches.

Drive shims between the logs on both sides of the planned opening to keep the sawed ends of the logs from sagging as you cut the opening.

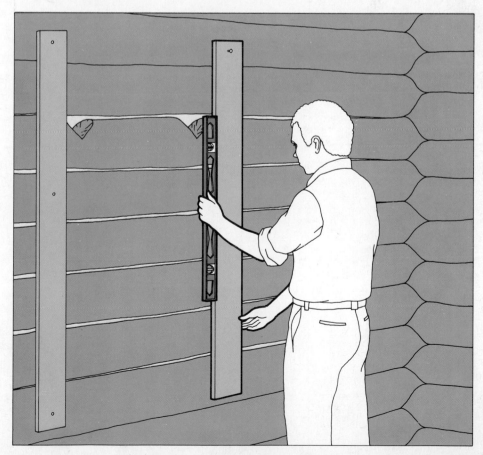

2 **Cutting out the openings.** Starting at the triangular starter notches *(page 56, Step 4)*, use a chain saw to cut along both guide strips to the top and bottom lines for each opening. Run the chain-saw blade flush with the interior and exterior strips to ensure a square cut; remove log sections one by one as you cut through them.

3 **Squaring the top and bottom.** Saw several vertical cuts to the marked top and bottom lines for the opening, then chisel away the waste wood and smooth the bottom surface with a drawknife. Make this surface flat for a window or a prehung door; slant it slightly down and outward for a homemade door *(page 63)*.

4 **Framing the openings.** Nail together rough frames of 2-by-8s, making them as wide as the opening and high enough to leave about 3 inches of air space above a doorframe and about 2 inches above a window frame. Rest the frames in the openings, inner edges flush with the inner wall, plumb the frames, and nail them temporarily in place.

Drill several linked holes through the side jambs with a $^7/_{16}$-inch bit to form vertical slots about 2 inches long, making two slots for each log end next to the jambs. Drive an 8-inch spike through the top of each slot to secure the frames *(inset)*, and remove the temporary nails.

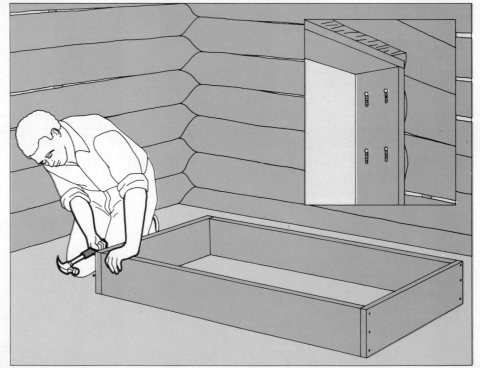

Fitting Logs for Gable and Roof

The techniques of building with logs change drastically at the gable and the roof. Walls can be built level, plumb and square in a piecemeal way, course by course; gables and roofs must be laid out as a whole to exact pitches. And because the work above the eaves is done high above the ground, where sharp, heavy tools are hard to manage, tinkering for a proper fit becomes impractical or downright dangerous. To avoid as much rooftop work as possible, all the rafters and gables are planned in advance, cut on the ground and assembled in place.

The first step in topping out a cabin is deciding the pitch of the roof. While roofs with little slope are lighter and faster to build, roofs in areas subject to heavy snowfall may need a steep pitch *(page 96)* and roofs sheathed with wooden shingles or shakes must be steep enough for good drainage *(page 74)*.

Having decided upon the pitch of your roof, you must cut rafters to match it. A jig fashioned from 1-by-8 boards will serve as a saw guide for two essential rafter cuts: the ridge cut, which joins the tops of rafters at the peak of a roof; and the bird's-mouth notch, which fits the underside of a rafter to the plate log at the top of a wall.

Choose the rafter logs carefully—from 5 to 6 inches thick and as smooth and straight as possible—and flatten their top faces with a chain saw *(page 54, Step 2)*. If a log is at all curved, install it with the convex arc of the curve facing upward; the log will straighten under the load of the roofing material above it.

1 **Plotting the roof line.** Tack an upright to the center of the gable wall, setting the top of the upright at least as high as the planned roof peak, and string lines from the upright to the plate logs to outline the angle of the roof. Using the line as a rough guide, scribe and notch the first log for the gable, and spike it in place.

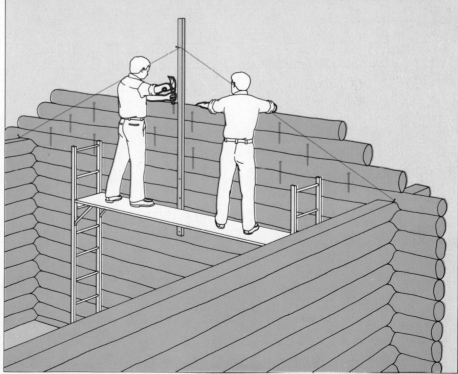

2 **Building the gables.** Drill spike holes through the gable logs every 2 feet and lift the logs into place one at a time, checking each log with a plumb bob and spiking it to the log below. Use short logs on the upper part of a wall, but be sure that the ends of every log extend beyond the guide strings. When the logs reach the level of the roof peak, remove the upright and strings.

3 **Planning the rafters.** Tack a 1-by-8 to the inside of the gable wall, with the lower edge of the board resting on the plate log and running up to the center of the wall at the planned angle of the roof. Snap a chalk line along the board 3 inches above its lower edge.

4 **Making a pattern for rafters.** Hold a level vertically against the outside face of the plate log and the 1-by-8, and draw a line along the level from the outer edge of the plate up to the chalk line on the 1-by-8. From the top of this vertical line draw a horizontal line all the way to the lower edge of the 1-by-8, completing the marks for a bird's-mouth notch.

Mark a ridge cut at the upper end of the 1-by-8 by snapping a vertical chalk line up the exact center of the gable wall, then extending the line across the 1-by-8. Take the 1-by-8 down, cut it along the marked lines and use it as a template to mark and cut a second 1-by-8.

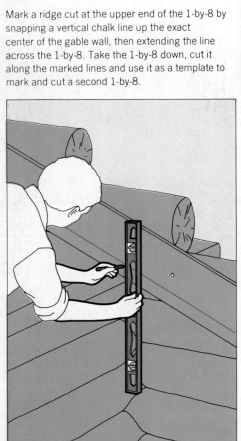

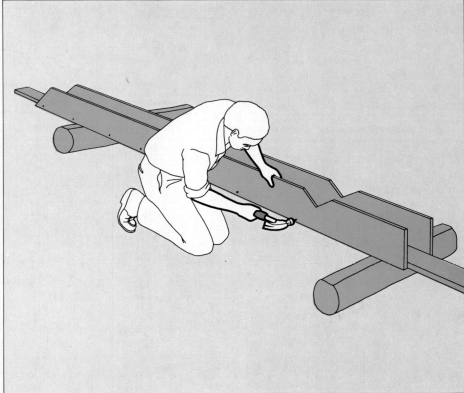

5 **Assembling the jig.** Nail the 1-by-8s, bird's-mouth notches up, to opposite edges of a long 2-by-6, aligning the ridge cuts and bird's-mouth notches of the 1-by-8s directly opposite each other. Secure the 2-by-6 to two scrap logs.

6 **Cutting the rafters.** After flattening the top face of a rafter pole with a chain saw, following the procedure on page 54, Step 2, secure the pole, flattened face down, in the jig with log dogs. Cut the bird's-mouth notch and bevel the ridge end of the pole with a bucksaw—a chain saw is not used because it might damage the jig—using the end and notch of the jig as saw guides. Saw off the lower end of the rafter or, if you prefer, trim it with an ax for a more rustic look, leaving at least 18 inches beyond the bird's-mouth for an overhang.

After cutting two rafters, raise them to opposite walls and rest them on the plate logs and a sturdy board laid across the top of the walls.

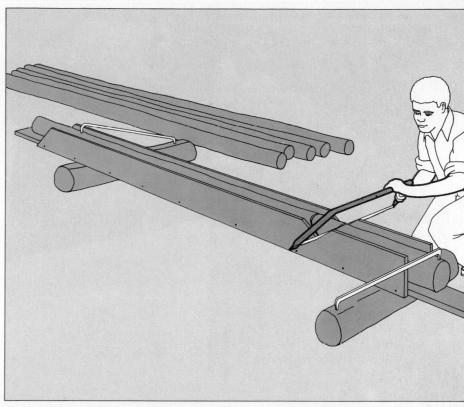

7 **Assembling a rafter pair.** Butt the ridge bevels of the rafters and nail a temporary horizontal brace across the rafter pair to hold the assembly tight for nailing, then drive four 8-inch spikes through the ridge at several angles (inset).

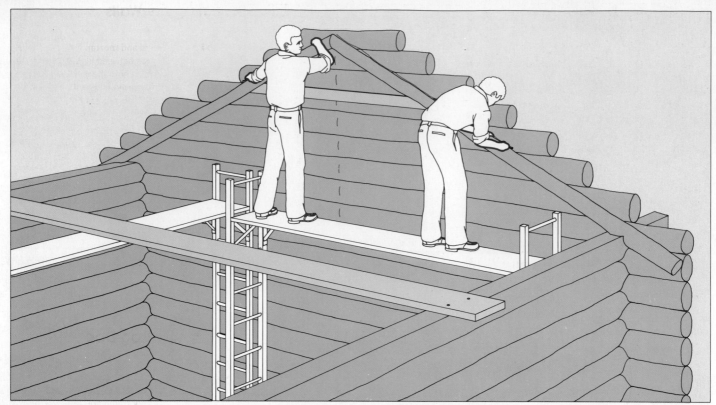

8 **Trimming the gable logs.** Hold the rafter pair against a gable wall, aligning the rafter peak with the center line you have chalked on the wall and fitting the bird's-mouth notches over the plate logs. (You may need to chisel some wood from a bird's-mouth or a plate log to bring the peak into line.) While a helper steadies the rafters, run a grease pencil along the top of each rafter to mark the gable wall for trimming. Remove the rafters, nail 2-by-4 guide strips just below the marked lines and run a saw along the guides to trim the ends of the logs.

9 **Installing the rafters.** Set the rafter pair on the ends of the plate logs, outside the gable wall, and drive spikes through the rafter and into the plate log at each bird's-mouth notch. Hang a plumb bob from the underside of the peak, push the rafters into plumb and nail a temporary brace between each rafter and the top of the gable wall. Assemble a second pair of rafters, use it to trim the opposite gable logs, then spike and brace it to the opposite ends of the plate logs.

String a line between the end peaks to serve as a guide for the peaks of the remaining rafters. Assemble these rafters, then spike, plumb and brace them roughly 24 inches apart for a roof of shakes nailed to spaced boards; for a roof sheathed with plywood, place the rafters on precise 16- or 24-inch centers. When you have installed all the rafters, lay a long, straight-edged board across them to detect high spots; trim these spots with a drawknife.

Making the Cabin Snug

After the roof for the cabin is finished, you must fill, or chink, all the gaps between the logs of the walls. Wherever logs fit tightly, caulking with lengths of tarred hemp, called oakum, is sufficient. Larger gaps must be closed with wood scraps covered by metal lath and mortar.

You must also install doors and windows. It is a simple job to install factory-made units, but most commercial doors look out of place against log walls. Many craftsmen prefer to build their own doors, facing them with log slabs—round-faced, flat-backed slices cut from the outsides of logs.

Sealing the Walls

Chinking with wood and mortar. Pack wood scraps into wide gaps between logs and nail metal lath over the scraps on both the inside and outside of the cabin, bowing the lath slightly inward. Cover the lath with a layer of mortar, sloping the mortar slightly outward on the outside of the walls to shed water.

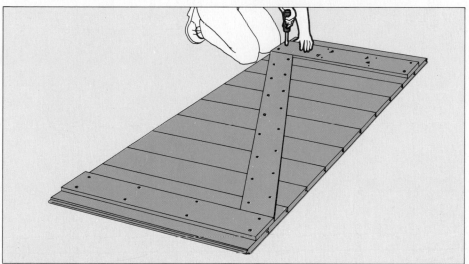

Making a Log Door

1 Making the base. Cut lengths of ¾-inch tongue-and-groove stock ¼ inch shorter than the width of the door frame and fit them together until they reach a length at least 1½ inches greater than the height of the door-frame. Screw a 1-by-6 Z brace to the back of the door, centering the horizontal legs of the brace over the seams between the last tongue-and-groove boards at top and bottom. Turn the door over and trim it ¼ inch shorter than the frame, removing the unused tongue and groove from the top and bottom boards, then staple building paper to the face of the door.

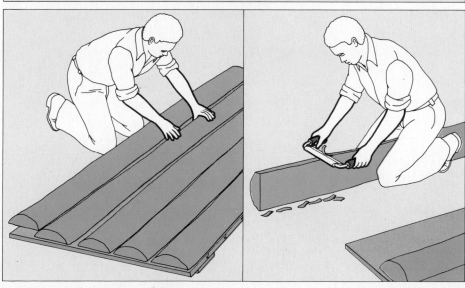

2 Finishing the door. Cut log slabs ¾ inch shorter than the height of the door, and trial-fit them vertically on the face of the door (*far left*), so they project slightly over the sides. Use a drawknife to trim the edges of the slabs (*near left*) until the entire slab assembly lies ¾ inch or less within the sides of the door. Nail the slabs to the face—use cut nails for a rustic appearance—with the slab ends flush with the bottom of the door. Hang the door in the rough frame (no finish frame is needed) with strap hinges, using 1-by-2s for doorstops.

A Cabin Suspended in a Cradle of Poles

Building a complete pole-frame cabin is not much different from erecting the basic platform described on pages 14-17. In each case, pressure-treated poles are planted in the ground and sturdy horizontal beams are bolted to them to support an understructure that serves as both foundation and floor.

The pole-frame cabin, of course, requires longer poles on the sides, to support additional beams for roof rafters or trusses. The result is a rustic vacation home that has even greater resistance to storms and floods than a structure that simply rests upon the platform.

A one-story cabin is built around two outside rows of 15-foot poles and one or more intermediate rows of 6- to 7-foot poles, all sunk and secured like those of a pole platform (*page 15, Steps 1-2*) and spaced no more than 8 feet apart. For a structure up to 16 feet wide, like the one illustrated, one middle row is needed and single 16-foot 2-by-10s serve as support beams. For a wider cabin requiring additional intermediate poles, you must span the width with beams in sections that are lapped at the intermediate poles (*page 16, Step 4*). To install the eave beams, use adjustable metal scaffolding, which can be rented. And because the high outer poles are so heavy and cumbersome, you should work with at least two helpers to set these poles into their holes.

After you have set the poles in the ground, the techniques of bracing and aligning them vary only slightly from those used for the pole platform. Plumb the inner surfaces of the side poles, using a 4-foot level and a longer piece of scrap wood for a straightedge; as you plumb each pole, leave the tapered side outward and brace each pole two thirds of the way up. When you cut daps (*page 15, Step 3*) in the side poles for floor beams, you will have to complete the recesses with a chisel. Cutting daps for the eave beams can be handled entirely with a saw. Once these supports are in place, your pole-frame cabin is ready to be roofed (*pages 67-73*) and walled.

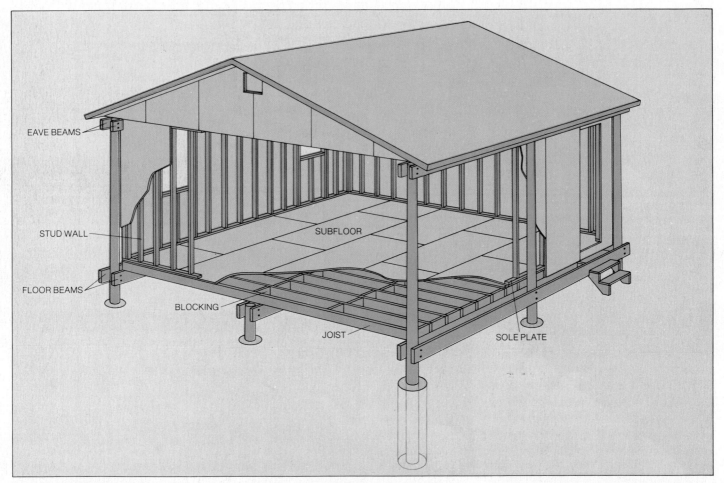

EAVE BEAMS

STUD WALL

FLOOR BEAMS

BLOCKING

SUBFLOOR

JOIST

SOLE PLATE

A cradle of high and low poles. Two outer rows of high poles and a middle row of short ones support and frame this cabin. Double 2-by-10 beams set in daps and bolted to each row of poles support the joists. Double 2-by-8s set in daps and bolted to the outside poles support the roof framing. Blocking—2-by-6s toenailed at right angles between joists every 4 feet—stabilizes the joists and provides a nailing surface for plywood subflooring. Because the walls support no weight, any kind of "curtain wall" can be used to enclose the cabin—this example has stud walls like those used to erect the frame cottage on pages 36-43. A prefabricated set of steps completes the exterior of the structure.

Building the Frame to the Eaves

1 Putting up the poles. For each outside pole, set a length of 2-by-10 into the hole, projecting about 10 inches aboveground. With two helpers, butt one pole end against the board and raise the other until the pole drops into the hole. Sink the middle poles and mark all poles for beams.

2 Attaching floor beams. Using a chisel to complete the daps, install the inner part of the double outer floor beams as for a platform (*page 16*). Next, use a combination square to measure across and mark the opposite side of each pole for the outer dap. Cut these daps with bucksaw and chisel, then attach the outer part of the beam, bolt the pole-beam sandwich together and install the middle floor beam.

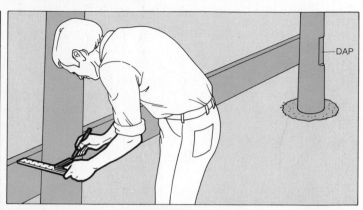

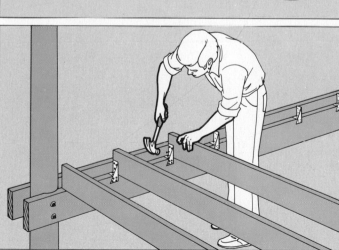

3 Installing joists. Beginning inside the corner poles at a distance equal to the thickness of the exterior sheathing, nail framing anchors every 16 inches to the inside beams and to one middle beam, and attach the joists. Nail blocking between joists and attach a subfloor.

4 Attaching eave beams. Measure up from the subfloor 8 feet to mark daps on the outside poles for double 2-by-8 eave beams. Then cut daps and attach beams to the outer rows of poles, following the procedures given for the floor beams of a platform (*pages 16-17*).

When a Cottage Was a Mansion

"Is this really America or have I landed on some enchanted isle?" exclaimed Grand Duke Boris of Russia in 1902 upon seeing the "cottages" of the Newport, R.I., seaside resort.

The Grand Duke was familiar with the sumptuous summer residences of Europe's rich in Cannes, Deauville and Biarritz, but Newport was altogether different. Running along the rocky Atlantic shore as far as the eye could see were estates that their owners, with audacious understatement, insisted on calling summer cottages. They were vacation homes of a splendor unmatched by any built before or since. Although occupied but 10 weeks a year, they were imperially scaled mansions of as many as a hundred rooms, and each of them cost millions of dollars to build.

At the turn of the century, homes like Commodore William Edgar's Sunny Wide Place (right, above) went up all over Newport as millionaires tried to outdo their neighbors. Sportsman Oliver H. P. Belmont built 52-room Belcourt Castle, which boasted a vaulted ballroom, stained-glass windows that were really doors leading onto balconies, and a towering fireplace topped with miniature battlements.

One of the most *nouveau* of the *nouveau riche* at Newport was Tessie Oelrichs, daughter of a Nevada miner who had struck it rich in the Comstock Lode. When she asked architect Stanford White to design "something special" for the summer season in Newport, he responded with a 40-room French Renaissance-style palace that she called Rosecliff. Behind its gleaming marble façade were the largest ballroom in the United States and a heart-shaped marble staircase around which hundreds of guests swirled. At one party—*le Bal Blanc*, or the White Ball—white swans floated in marble pools while a dozen white-hulled ships, specially built for

the occasion, were anchored offshore.

Sumptuous though they were, the Belmont and Oelrichs places were overshadowed by the most opulent of all Newport's cottages—the huge Italian Renaissance-style palace that railroad mogul Cornelius Vanderbilt called The Breakers. Appropriately, The Breakers had its origin in a spirit—indeed, a passion—of competition. Mrs. Vanderbilt wanted to upstage her sister-in-law, whose husband had spent two million dollars to erect the neo-classical Marble House and another nine million dollars for an interior that included solid-bronze furniture, a ballroom paneled in gold and a dining room sheathed in Algerian marble.

Mrs. Vanderbilt's sister-in-law got her comeuppance as The Breakers slowly rose beside the sea. Five stories high and built of close-cut stone, the Vanderbilt "cottage" sat in 11 manicured acres on a small promontory jutting out into the Atlantic. The house cost five million dollars—a truly fabulous sum at a time when laborers earned a dollar a day—and it took two years to complete. As it went up, interior decorators and an army of workers struggled with the tons of paneling, gilt, statuary, wrought

iron, brass and bronze arriving each week from France and Italy.

Tapestries, fireplaces (one inscribed with the motto, "Little do I care for wealth") and rare alabaster pillars were taken from the estates of impoverished European noblemen. Everything in the grand salon—walls, gilding, furniture—was built in France by master craftsmen who then traveled to Newport to supervise the installation.

Bathrooms at The Breakers had sinks with solid-silver faucets that spewed hot and cold fresh water and hot and cold sea water; bathtubs were carved from blocks of solid marble. There were 70 rooms all told, of which 33 were reserved for a huge staff of summer servants. Some 150 tons of coal were used to heat the building every winter, though it was occupied at that season by only a handful of servants.

Though all this grandiose construction produced a confusing potpourri of buildings that ranged from French chateaux to English Tudor mansions, Newport's monumental cottages did magnificently what their creators—a clutch of millionaires and a pantheon of American architects—set out to do: overwhelm everyone who saw them.

Practical Shortcuts to a Strong Framed Roof

A roof frame of rafters in either shed or gable style makes an appropriately simple topping for the simple structures described in this book. A shed roof, a single deck that slants from a high wall on one side of a building to a low wall at the other, is especially easy to build. Each rafter extends over the whole width of the building, and the rafters must be thick and heavy if the distance is long. A gable roof, which rises from both walls to a central ridge beam, divides the distance in two. It takes longer to build, but it permits the use of lighter and less expensive stock for rafters—or even prefabricated rafter sets called trusses (*pages 72-73*)—and thus is a more common choice for the roofs of large cabins.

For both shed and gable roofs, the long boards used as rafters must be cut at angles to fit the top plates of walls, the ridge of a roof or the overhang of an eave. Where a rafter rests upon a top plate, it will need the notch called a bird's-mouth to hold it securely. Where it meets a ridge beam, it will need a bevel called a ridge cut. Rafter ends that overhang beyond a wall are generally cut off parallel to the wall so that trim boards can be nailed to their ends. Cutting the special angles for top plates, ridge beams and overhangs can be a tricky business in large, complex roofs, but for the simple frames shown here they can be cut without intricate calculations or special tools.

Before you cut the rafters, you must decide upon the pitch, or slope, of your roof. The decision is largely a matter of esthetics, except that certain roof coverings require a specified minimum pitch. Wood shakes or shingles, for instance, must be laid atop a roof that rises at least 4 inches for each foot of horizontal distance below it; metal panels or asphalt shingles can be laid at a minimum pitch of 2 inches per foot.

The distance between wall tops in a shed roof, or between a wall top and the ridge beam in a gable roof, is the span of the rafter. Most rafters are in fact longer than their span, to provide an overhang beyond the wall tops, but it is the span that determines the stock from which a rafter is cut. Ordinary rafters spaced on 16-inch centers—normal for frame construction—should be cut from 2-by-4s for spans up to 5 feet, 2-by-6s up to 9 feet, 2-by-8s up to 11 feet, 2-by-10s up to 14 feet, and 2-by-12s up to 18 feet. Rafters spaced on 24-inch centers should be 2-by-6s for spans up to 6½ feet, 2-by-8s up to 9½ feet, 2-by-10s up to 12 feet, and 2-by-12s up to 15½ feet. (For roofs that must bear a heavy load of snow, see the chart on page 97.) If you are building a gable roof, you also will need a supply of joist stock: the walls beneath a gable roof must be tied together by ceiling joists to prevent the rafters from splaying or sagging.

Framing a Shed Roof

1 Marking the bird's-mouth cut. Snap a chalk line down the middle of a rafter board and hold the board against the end of the building so that the chalk line touches the top plates of the high and low walls. Tack the board to the plates and mark the board at the top and outside edges of the lower top plate; extend the horizontal line at the top of the plate to the bottom edge of the board. At the high wall, mark along the inside face of the top plate, across the top of the top plate and to the edge of the board.

2 Marking the overhang cuts. Place a carpenter's level against the rafter board at the point you have chosen for the end of the overhang and draw a plumb line to mark the overhang cut. Remove the rafter board and cut it along the marks, then use this rafter as a template to cut the remaining rafters. Mark the high and low top plates for rafters on 16- or 24-inch centers and attach metal rafter anchors at the left edges of the rafter locations on the upper plate, at the right edges on the lower plate; for the two end rafters, attach both anchors to the locations of the inner face of the rafter.

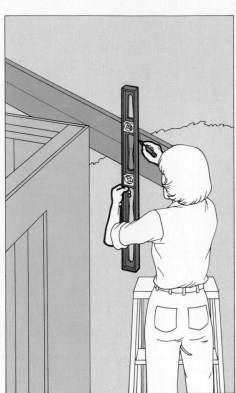

3 Attaching the rafters. Set the rafters against the rafter anchors, fitting the bird's-mouth notches snugly over the top plates, and nail the rafters in place. On the two top plates of the other walls, which run parallel to the rafters, mark locations for cripple-studs 3½ inches wide, centered above each wall stud.

4 Installing cripple studs. Working from inside the structure, hold a 2-by-4 flat against the outside of the top plate and the end rafter at each marked location. Plumb each 2-by-4 and mark it along the top plate and the bottom edge of the rafter, then cut the 2-by-4s at the marks and toenail them to the plate and rafter.

Framing a Gable Roof

1 Installing joists. Toenail joists, cut to span the width of the cabin, to the top plates of the side walls on either 16- or 24-inch centers, matching the planned spacing of the studs; locate the two end joists 1½ inches from the outside of the gable-wall top plates.

If the structure has an interior partition running across the joists, like the frame cottage on pages 36-43, you can use joists only half as long as the width of the cabin. Butt the inner ends of these joists over the partition, toenail them to the partition's top plate and tie them together with metal gussets, called truss plates *(inset)*.

2 Making temporary ridge-beam supports. Nail 1-by-2 cleats 1½ inches apart (the thickness of a 2-by-8 ridge beam) to protrude beyond the ends of two 1-by-6 temporary supports. Center and nail an assembled support to the inside of each end joist, with the top of the support 7½ inches lower than the planned height of the roof peak. Install diagonal braces between each support and an end joist. Cut a 2-by-8 ridge beam to the length of the cabin and mark it for rafters on either 16- or 24-inch centers.

3 Raising the ridge beam. With a helper, center the ridge beam in the temporary supports. Snap a chalk line down the middle of a rafter board that is long enough to reach from the ridge beam to the top plate, plus any planned overhang.

4 Marking the ridge cut. With a helper, set the rafter board against the gable wall, with the outside edge of the top plate touching the chalk line and the top edge of the ridge beam touching the top of the rafter. Tack the rafter in place, mark a vertical ridge cut down the rafter board along the face of the ridge beam, then mark the bird's-mouth and overhang cuts as shown on pages 67-68, Steps 1 and 2.

Cut the rafter at the marked lines and use it as a template to mark and cut the remaining rafters. Nail metal rafter anchors to the top plates next to all but the end joists, positioning them for rafters set against the ends of the joists. Mark the ridge beam for corresponding rafter locations.

5 **Nailing the rafters.** While one helper holds a rafter to the location mark at one end of the ridge beam and another holds it to the top plate, butt-nail the ridge beam to the rafter. Nail the other end of the rafter to the joist with four 10-penny nails. Toenail a second rafter to the ridge beam opposite the first, and secure it to the top plate in the same way. Attach a second pair of rafters at the other end of the ridge beam and fill in the remaining pairs of rafters along the beam, fastening each rafter to the ridge beam, to a joist and to a metal rafter anchor.

6 **Trimming the joists.** With a circular saw, trim the corners of each joist flush with the top of the rafters, using the edge of the rafter as a guide for the saw blade. Remove the temporary ridge-beam supports and attach cripple studs to the gable walls (*page 68, Step 4*).

Assembling a Set of Trusses

The easiest way to frame a conventional gable roof is to use a set of factory-built trusses, which eliminates the tricky jobs of installing a ridge beam and cutting angles in rafters. The trusses—zigzags of 2-by-4s fastened with toothed metal plates—span distances as great as 40 feet without a load-bearing interior partition. Upper timbers called chords take the place of carefully cut rafters, while a bottom chord serves as the ceiling joist. Diagonal "webs" connect the top and bottom chords, transferring weight to the beams or top plates of the building. End-truss webs run vertically to accommodate sheathing and a ventilator.

When ordering trusses, specify the span between front- and back-wall top plates or eave beams, the length of overhang at the eaves, the size of the ventilator opening and the pitch, or slope, you want for the roof—generally at least 4 inches of rise for every foot of horizontal span. You will need adjustable scaffolding, available at rental agencies.

1 Fastening the nailers. Attach framing anchors every 24 inches along the top plates (or, for a pole-frame cabin, eave beams) of the front and back walls; for the gable-end walls, nail 2-by-4 nailers to the plates 1½ inches in from the outside edges. The 1½-inch offset is handily gauged by holding a 2-by-4 block on edge and flush with the outside edge of the plates. Align the ends of the nailers with the outside edges of the front and back top plates.

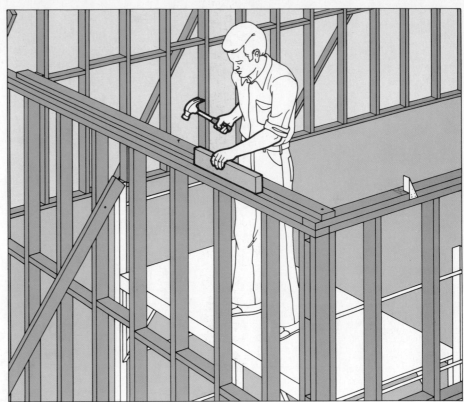

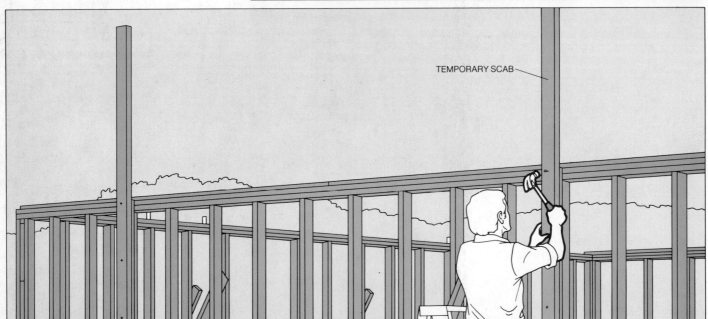

TEMPORARY SCAB

2 Erecting temporary scabs. To make scabs—needed to brace the end trusses—nail four 4-foot strips of the sheathing you will use for the cabin, to four 8-foot 2-by-4s. Nail two scabs to studs in each end wall about a third of the way in from front and back walls, with the sheathed half of each scab below the top plates. (For a pole-frame cabin [*pages 64-65*], where the roof is framed before the walls, make scabs of unsheathed 2-by-4s extending from the ground to 4 feet above the eave beams. Set them flush with each end of the cabin and brace them.)

Sheathe the end trusses with plywood and cut a ventilator opening in the sheathing.

3 **Rolling the trusses.** Working with two helpers on scaffolding, set the ends of an end truss upside down on the top plates of the front and back walls and, with a 2-by-4 wedged into its peak, push the truss upright to the helpers. Walk the truss to the end wall, set it into position between the nailer and the scabs, and nail the scabs to the top chords and the nailer to the bottom chord.

4 **Bracing the trusses.** Roll up the second truss following the same procedure as for the end truss and nail it to the framing anchors on the front and back walls. Temporarily brace the second truss to the end truss with a 1-by-6 marked at 2-foot intervals and nailed to the top chords of both trusses. Nail a second marked 1-by-6 to the top chord on the other side of the ridge. Install the other trusses in the same way; where 1-by-6 braces adjoin, lap them over two trusses.

5 **Plumbing the trusses.** Loosen the scabs on an end truss, nail a long diagonal 2-by-4 brace to the ventilator framing and plumb the truss with a mason's level. Once it is plumb, have a helper nail the brace to a stake. Fasten sheets of exterior-grade plywood atop the trusses, removing the 1-by-6 braces as you work. Then nail the 1-by-6s across the tops of the bottom chords to link the chords and add stability. If your structure is in a high-wind area, add 1-by-6 diagonal braces between the webs of each end truss and the bottom chord of the fifth truss from each end wall. Remove the temporary scabs.

Covering the Roof: Shingles, Shakes and Panels

Most cabins, like most houses, are roofed with asphalt shingles *(page 76)*, but two somewhat less common materials should be given special consideration: wooden shakes and corrugated metal. Shakes *(pages 76-77)*, though expensive, provide the most appropriately rustic covering. Metal offers very practical advantages: economy, easy installation, fire resistance and, for areas subject to heavy snow, a slippery surface that sheds snow before it can build up.

The type of metal roofing illustrated on the following pages—called 5-V crimp because each panel has pairs of V-shaped corrugations, or crimps, at the sides and a single crimp in the middle—is particularly simple to work with. It is available at most large farm-equipment and building-supply dealers in panels 5 to 12 feet long, in a variety of colors, in both aluminum and galvanized steel—aluminum is recommended for amateur builders because it is both light in weight and easy to cut and bend. Unlike other kinds of metal roofing, 5-V crimp does not require separate moldings at the eaves. The only special trim that you will need is a ridge roll—a rounded piece of aluminum sheet with flanges—to cap the roof ridge.

The 5-V crimp material can be used on roofs that have a pitch of at least 2 inches of rise in each 12 inches of horizontal span. Shakes require a pitch of at least 4 in 12, asphalt shingles 2 in 12. Roofs of lower pitch are difficult to make weather-tight without professionally applied "built-up" roofing. The methods illustrated on the following pages, simplified from those prescribed for year-round homes, are suitable for vacation and weekend cottages in moderate climates; in areas subject to severe icing and heavy snow, additional weatherproofing such as flashing *(page 97)* may be advisable.

A Snow-shedding Surface of Aluminum

1 **Preparing an end panel.** After installing a roof deck—generally ½-inch, type C-D plywood in rows with staggered joints—and fascia boards, use tin snips to trim off the two outer Vs from one side of an end panel. Then make tabs to bend over the eave and gable by snipping 1-inch slits 1 inch in from each trimmed corner; snip similar slits into each fold of the three Vs remaining.

EAVE EDGE

CROWN

GABLE EDGE

2 Installing the first end panel. Starting from the end opposite the direction of prevailing winds, position the end panel so its slits are flush with the gable and eave edges of the roof, nail the middle V through the crown at two-foot intervals and fold down the edges of the panel. Drive roofing nails—the kind sold with attached neoprene washers—through the folded-down edges into the roof fascia boards at 6-inch intervals. Fold over and nail down the small tabs snipped at the Vs to close the ends of each V.

3 Installing intermediate panels. Working on the ground, slit the Vs at the eave edge as in Step 1. Then, on the roof, overlap the double Vs of the second panel with the Vs of the end panel; nail at the crown of each V at 1-foot intervals, and bend and nail the eave edge of the panel.

Add the remaining panels of the course in the same way along the eaves until you come close enough to the other end for its end panel, which is cut to fit and attached in the same way as the first end panel (Steps 1 and 2). Add additional courses up the roof as necessary, overlapping them at least one foot and trimming and bending the end panels. At the ridge, nail into the valleys—the space between double Vs— and hammer all Vs flat 6 inches down from the ridge to make a surface for the ridge roll.

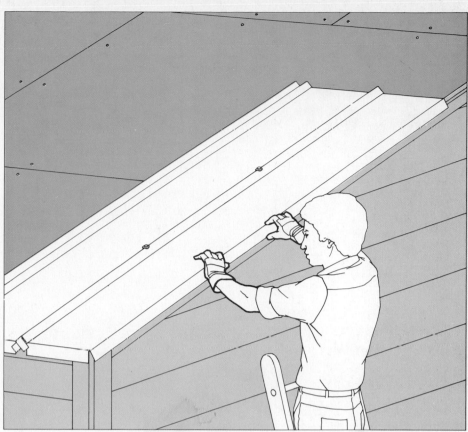

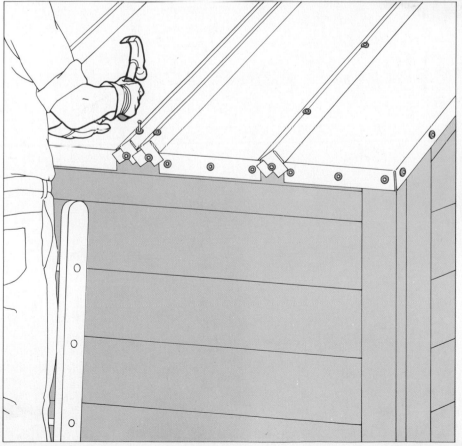

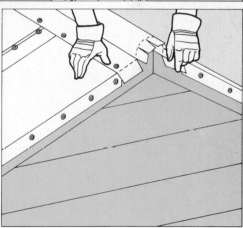

4 Attaching the ridge roll. With tin snips, make 3-inch tabs in the rounded top of the ridge roll, at the ends that will fit over the gable peaks. Nail the flanges of the roll every 6 inches over the flattened Vs of the panels, and fold the tabs to close the roll ends. Fold the flange ends over, and nail them and the tabs to the fascia.

An Asphalt-Shingle Roof

Laying a pattern. In this simplified installation of asphalt shingles (a single shingle is shown in the inset), a ½-inch, type C-D plywood deck is laid with staggered joints and covered with 15-pound roofing felt overlapped 6 inches at the bottom edges. Fascia boards are not essential. If ice may be a problem, add flashing (*page 97*).

Along the eaves, lay a starter course of shingles from which 3 inches have been cut off the left edge; these first pieces laid should also have the three tabs trimmed off. Place the first course of untrimmed shingles over the starter course, and overhanging the eaves and gables ½ inch. Apply courses above so the lower edge of each shingle lies directly over the top of the cutouts of the one lower down. Begin the second course with a shingle trimmed by 4 inches at one end and begin the third course with a shingle trimmed by 8 inches (*broken lines*). The fourth course is the same as the first, the fifth the same as the second and so on to the ridge.

The ridge is finished with individual shingle tabs, bent to cover both sides. Start the job by nailing a tab at each end of the roof ½ inch beyond the gable to match the shingle overhang; overlap succeeding tabs 7 inches.

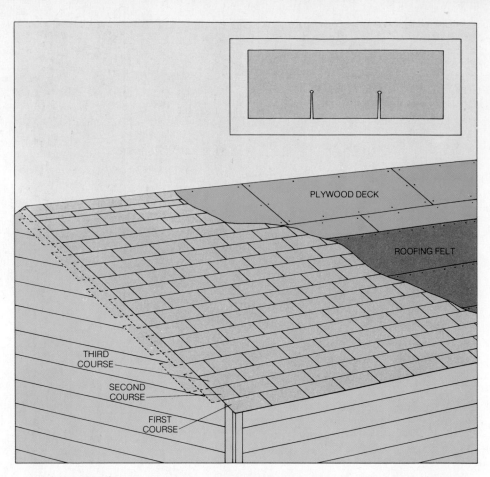

PLYWOOD DECK

ROOFING FELT

THIRD COURSE

SECOND COURSE

FIRST COURSE

Laying a Shake Roof

1 Covering the edge. Shakes are traditionally laid over an open deck of 1-by-3 boards nailed to the rafters and, for the 16-inch shakes illustrated, centers spaced 7 inches apart—except for the lowest two rows, whose centers are 5½ inches apart. Lay the starter course so that the shakes overhang the eave by 2 inches and the gable by 1½ inches; space them ¼ inch apart and drive two nails per shake 9 inches from the bottom. Lay the first course right over the starter course, starting with a shake cut in half so that vertical joints are staggered by at least 1½ inches.

HALF-WIDTH SHAKE

FIRST COURSE

STARTER COURSE

2 **Laying remaining courses.** Lay each shake to overlap the top 9 inches of the shakes under it. Overhang 1½ inches at the gables. Drive nails 8½ inches above the bottom so that all nails are covered. Lay the final courses at the ridge so that the top edges of alternate shakes on one side of the roof butt against the undersides of the shakes on the other side (*inset*).

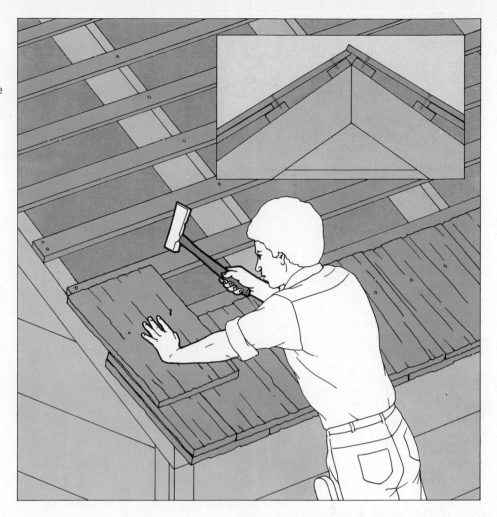

How to Split Shakes with a Frow and a Mallet

If you have a few cedar or redwood logs, you can make your own shakes fairly simply with a special cutting tool—available from specialty-tool suppliers—called a frow. Saw each log into 16-inch sections and mark off ¼-inch intervals across the top of the section for each shake. Place the log section on sturdy supports, hold the frow firmly—with its sharp edge against the top of the log—and strike the frow sharply with a wooden mallet.

The log should split evenly and the shake pop free of the log, though you will probably need several attempts to discover the necessary force and rhythm. Do not try to split through a knot; instead, remove the frow and start at the next mark on the log.

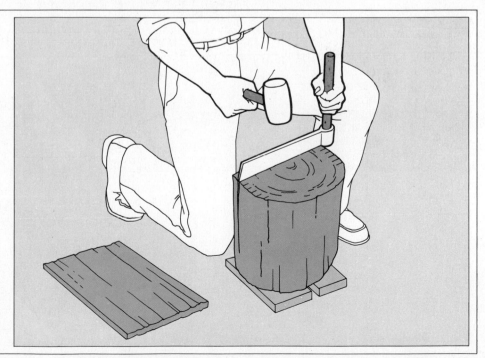

3

Making the Best of Nature's Worst

Special materials for special hazards. The oddly shaped masonry block at top, technically called a speed block, is designed to accommodate the vertical and horizontal reinforcing bars that stiffen the foundation of a cabin built in earthquake country *(pages 90-93)*. In an area of high wind, steel strapping and plates are fastened to the structure with ordinary galvanized nails, strengthening the vulnerable joints between joists, studs and rafters *(pages 86-89)*.

People who build vacation cabins seem deliberately to choose bad building sites: they seek land that is covered with deep snow in winter because they like to ski; they choose sites with the steep hills that invite erosion and washouts in order to enjoy rugged terrain or a stunning view; they select open land along the sea, where windstorms—which can tear the roof off a building—gather force as they blow over expanses of water.

On these less-than-ideal sites, safety can sometimes be built right into the structure. A cabin that is in the path of down-rushing water may be built high and dry with a pole foundation *(pages 80-85)*; one vulnerable to wind may be tied together with metal strapping at all its joints *(pages 86-89)* to resist dangerous gusts. In snow country, a cabin may have a roof with an especially steep pitch to shed snow before it accumulates to a dangerous weight *(page 97)*.

Some of these hazards may be better dealt with by working on the land than by employing special building techniques. On a breezy site, one to three rows of black spruce or black pine—Japanese black pine in coastal areas—will make an efficient and attractive windscreen. Leave a space between the trees so the rows break the force of the wind; rows that are planted too closely together will deflect the wind up and over the treetops, creating fierce eddies on the leeward side. A louvered fence, its slats oriented at an angle to the wind, can funnel wind around a cabin, and a deck or patio built on the lee side will be washed by a cool, filtered breeze all summer. Outbuildings, too, can serve double duty as windscreens if they are built on the windward side—generally the west or northwest side—of a cabin. Windward screens and outbuildings will also help to control snow; the winter wind will force the flakes against the wind block and keep them from drifting deep against the main building.

Simple improvements of a building site also can keep rushing streams of storm water from washing out hillsides or foundation pilings. With a few hours of shovel work, for example, you can sculpt hillside land with a series of shallow drainage channels, called swales, to turn aside the flow. Pile the dirt from the channels on the downhill side to make a lip, or berm, that will further help trap the water. To slow the velocity of the water without redirecting it, install baffles across a hill; the easiest ones are simply railroad ties, half-buried in a shallow trench and spiked down with long steel pins. Some leafy ground-cover plants also will help to slow flowing water, and the tough roots of some species will even hold soil against erosion. Pachysandra and English ivy are good choices throughout the East; dune grass is particularly hardy in seaside regions; dichondra thrives in desert and mountain areas.

A Firm Foundation for a Hillside Hideaway

Many a vacation cabin perches on the slope of a hill or the side of a mountain. The view is often breathtaking—and the lot is generally cheaper than a level one. Though any of the foundations described in Chapter 1 of this book can be built on such a site, a pole platform is the easiest to erect. Using methods adapted from those on pages 14-17, and working from scaffolds adjusted to the slope (opposite, top), you can set rows of poles rising to different heights above the ground in order to support a level platform on which to build a cabin.

The first adaptation you must make is in the size of the holes in which you sink the poles: sloping sites call for especially deep and wide holes, specified in the chart below. If the soil is deep enough for you to reach about 1½ feet below the correct depth but large rocks made digging difficult, you can simplify the job with a pole necklace—a concrete collar 12 inches thick, set around the pole (opposite, bottom). Using the necklace, you need to dig a hole of the required width only a foot below the frost line, then go down to the increased depth with a narrower hole. The pole will have as much strength as one with a soil-and-cement jacket of the required width, but the hole is much easier to dig.

Sometimes, however, the soil cover on a slope may be so shallow that you cannot reach the required depth. In that situation, consult a structural engineer. He may advise you that drilling into bedrock—a job best done by professionals—is the only way to anchor the poles.

Where drilling is not required, you can use the easier and less expensive anchoring techniques shown on pages 82-85. In this method the row of poles across the top of the slope is replaced by a masonry foundation wall called a key wall, and the downhill poles are secured in the shallow soil by concrete pads.

The key wall is the crucial element in the design; while the poles merely support the platform from below, the wall anchors both poles and platform against the pull of gravity downslope. Design your key wall with the help of a professional who is familiar with local soil conditions. One of his main concerns will be to show you how to channel the flow of water downhill so that it does not undermine the wall. Part of the solution to this problem is built right into the wall and its footing, in the form of passages, called weep holes, that let water pass through the masonry structure (pages 82 and 83, Steps 2 and 4). You also will probably have to preserve or replant vegetation to prevent erosion, and dig a gully uphill from the building site to channel runoff water around the key wall.

After building the wall and setting the poles, make a final adaptation of the basic pole-platform technique. Diagonal braces (page 85, Steps 8 and 9) must run within each row of poles across the slope and from row to row up the slope to keep the poles from slipping or racking above their shallow holes.

A Hole for Every Soil and Site

Pole height (in feet)	1½-3	1½-3	3-8	9-20		
Slope	less than 1:10	1:10-1:1		1:3	1:2	1:1
Good soil	4' by 18"	4½' by 18"	5½' by 18"	4' by 18"	4' by 18"	6' by 18"
Average soil	4' by 24"	6' by 24"	7' by 24"	4' by 24"	5' by 24"	7' by 24"
Below-average soil	5' by 36"	8' by 36"	—	4½' by 36"	6' by 36"	—

Choosing hole dimensions. The figures in this chart indicate the depth (in feet) and width (in inches) of the holes required for platform poles that are 7 to 9 inches thick and set 8 feet apart on a sloping site. These figures vary with the height of the pole aboveground, the steepness of the slope and the quality of the soil. Though the hole dimensions provide good guides for a variety of situations, check the dimensions for your site with a structural engineer.

Relatively short poles, generally near the top of the site, are covered in the first three vertical columns of the chart; higher poles in the last three. Slopes are given in civil engineer's notation, as ratios; a slope of 1:10, for example, has a 1-foot rise in every 10 horizontal feet. Soils are classified by their composition: good soil consists of compact sand, gravel or hard clay; average soil, of loose gravel or compacted clay; below-average soil, of soft clay, clay with large amounts of silt, or loosely compacted sand.

To use the chart, match the height of a pole to the slope of the site to locate the correct vertical column, then read down the column to the horizontal row that matches the quality of your soil; the intersection of the column and row gives the dimensions of the required hole. For example, a pole 7 feet high, on a site with a slope of 1:3 and average soil, needs a hole 7 feet deep and 24 inches wide. Note that two spaces in the chart contain dashes rather than dimensions. These situations, characterized by steep slopes and below-average soils, require holes so large that digging them becomes impractical.

How to Level a Scaffold

Fitting the uprights to the site. To make flat supports for the uprights of a scaffold, wedge 3-foot lengths of 2-by-4 into the ground at the uphill and downhill points you have chosen for the uprights; if necessary, clear out some soil to make the tops of the 2-by-4s level. Stack additional 2-by-4s upon the two bases to reach a height that is level with the ground 7 inches uphill, then set level lengths of 2-by-8s between the stacked 2-by-4s and the ground. In poor soil, drive stakes at the downhill edges of these lumber levelers. Remove the wheels from the scaffold uprights, set the uprights on the wooden bases you have made and fit the platform supports to the position holes of the uprights that will make the platform level.

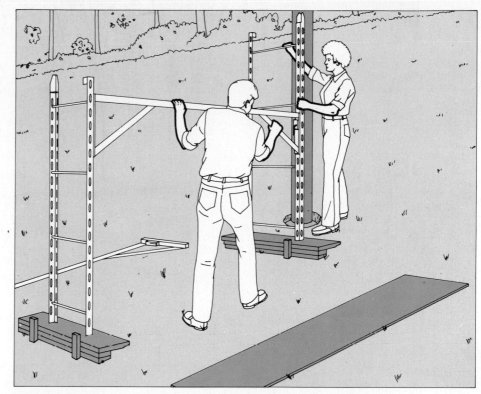

A Necklace for Stony Soil

Making a pole necklace. Dig a hole of the diameter called for in the chart on the opposite page, down to a foot below the frost line, then reduce the width of the hole to 14 inches and extend it down 1½ feet below the depth called for in the chart *(near right)*. Set eight evenly spaced ½-inch lag bolts in a ring around the pole at a point that will be 6 inches below the frost line, with the bolt heads protruding 6 inches from the surface of the pole. When you have braced the pole in place, fill the narrow part of the hole with earth and fill the wider part, up to the frost line, with concrete *(far right)*. After the concrete has hardened, fill the hole above the concrete necklace with a final layer of earth.

A Wall and Pads for Shallow Soil

1 Digging the key-wall footing. Locate the building lines (*pages 26-27, Steps 1 and 2*), then dig a trench 3 feet deep and 16 inches wide just outside the line you have established across the top of the slope. Undercut the downhill edge of the trench slightly, so that the bottom of the trench is wider than the top.

2 Making weep holes for the trench. At 4-foot intervals, dig pockets 3 inches wide and 4 inches deep into opposite sides of the trench, halfway up from the bottom. Insert a length of 1½-inch rigid plastic pipe, capped at one end with galvanized mesh, into each pair of pockets, with the capped end in the uphill pocket. Run two lengths of reinforcing bar along the trench, securing them to the plastic pipes with tie wire.

3 Starting the key wall. Restring the building lines, pour concrete up to the downhill edge of the trench and push a masonry block 2 inches into the concrete, using the building lines as guides. Lay two more blocks of this course.

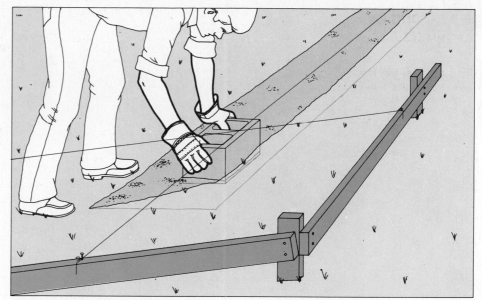

4 Making weep holes in the wall. At the fourth block position, lay a hollow-core partition block on its side and a half-height block atop it. Complete the first course, laying hollow-core partition and half-height blocks at every fourth block position, and install joint reinforcement over the top of the course (page 28, Step 2).

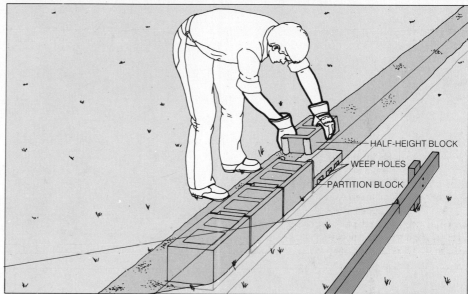

HALF-HEIGHT BLOCK

WEEP HOLES

PARTITION BLOCK

5 Finishing the wall. Sink a reinforcing bar through one core of each block, with the bottom of the reinforcing bar about 2 feet into the footing and the top protruding 14 inches above the top of the block, then let the concrete harden. Beginning with a half block, lay a second course of regular blocks; then lay a third course of regular blocks alone. Fill the hollow cores of all the blocks down to the footing with concrete, and install a sill plate and a header joist as you would on a continuous foundation wall (page 30, Step 1, and page 31, Steps 1 and 2).

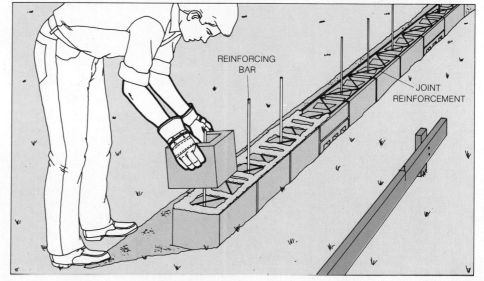

REINFORCING BAR

JOINT REINFORCEMENT

6 **Setting the poles.** After digging holes at the pole locations, pour a concrete pad 4 inches deep in the bottom of each hole and sink the pole 2 inches into the wet concrete; to set a pole longer than 8 feet, use the method shown on page 65, Step 1. Align, plumb and brace the pole immediately (*page 15, Step 2*), let the pad dry for a day, then fill the hole with soil.

7 **Putting in the joists.** Install double floor beams (*pages 15-17*) parallel to the key wall and set the floor joists in place. Fasten these joists to the beams by the techniques shown on page 17, Step 7; and to the sill and header joist by the techniques on page 31, Step 3.

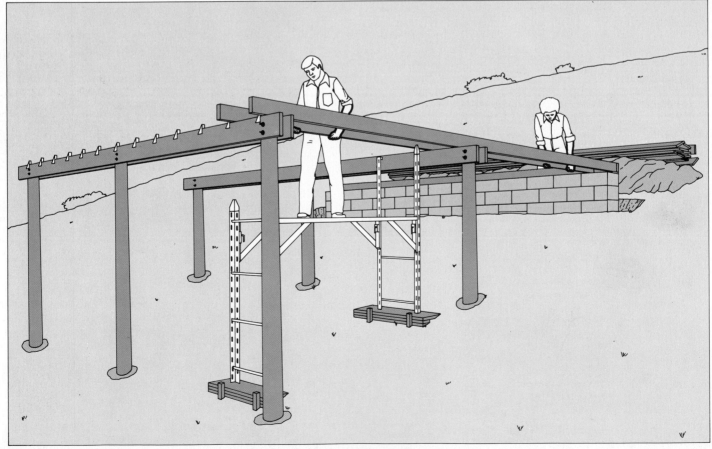

8 **Bracing the poles laterally.** To secure a row of three poles across the bottom of the slope, fasten 2-by-4 braces running from the bottoms of the outside poles to points on the inner surface of a floor beam near the middle pole, using two lag bolts at each connection. On the opposite side of the same row, fasten a brace running from the bottom of the middle pole to a point on the inside surface of thc other floor beam, close to either of the outside poles.

9 **Bracing the poles uphill.** Fasten braces between the bottoms of the longer poles and the tops of the shorter poles, just below the floor beams. Brace the bottom of each shorter pole to a joist at a point near the key wall.

Tying a House Together against the Wind

On September 22, 1938, after one of the worst hurricanes in American history, a newspaper reporter in Horseneck, Massachusetts, wrote of the "wasteland of sand and stone" that 48 hours earlier had been a town. He described "miles of summer places—from small cottages to large residences—smashed from their foundations." The destruction of the resort area was all but total—yet, if only they had been properly reinforced or anchored, many of the summer homes there might have withstood the 100- to 130-mph winds of that terrible storm.

A cabin is most vulnerable to wind damage—and, in an area that is subject to high winds, should be reinforced—at the joints between the foundation, floor and wall, and at the joints between the wall and roof. Some of the reinforcing techniques that are described on the following pages must be used as you build a frame structure; the other techniques can be used if you must strengthen an existing structure.

To reinforce the vulnerable points of a structure as you build, strengthen the joints with 1-inch 24-gauge galvanized-steel strapping, which is available at most hardware stores. The strapping comes with prepunched holes for nails or bolts, and can be cut with a pair of metal shears. Check with local building officials before you install it: many codes permit strapping at every other stud or joist, but in some high-wind areas codes may require you to strap every joint.

Your local code may also require you to install diagonal reinforcements to protect stud walls against winds that can rack a wall out of square. Traditionally, these reinforcements have consisted of "let-in" bracing—1-by-4s or 1-by-6s recessed, or let in, to notches cut in the studs. Many codes now permit the use of metal braces, available from building suppliers, which serve the same function but are nailed directly to the studs, eliminating the tedious job of notching each stud by hand.

On existing structures, strapping cannot be conveniently applied to exposed studs, joists or rafters, but there is a variety of steel connectors and plates, installed over the siding (page 88, top), that can be used to strengthen some vulnerable joints. Another method for keeping a roof on a cabin and a cabin on its foundation is, literally, to tie the structure to the ground with steel cables that are anchored to deadmen: 5-foot timbers buried permanently in the ground (page 89). As an emergency measure before a storm hits, you can also secure a roof with sandbags.

Regardless of how you reinforce your cabin in a high-wind area, always board up the windows when a bad storm threatens, leaving one or two windows slightly open on the lee side of the house to equalize the air pressure inside and out. During a hurricane the air outside the house is a low-pressure area, and higher air pressure indoors can burst doors and windows out of their frames.

Reinforcing a Cottage as You Build It

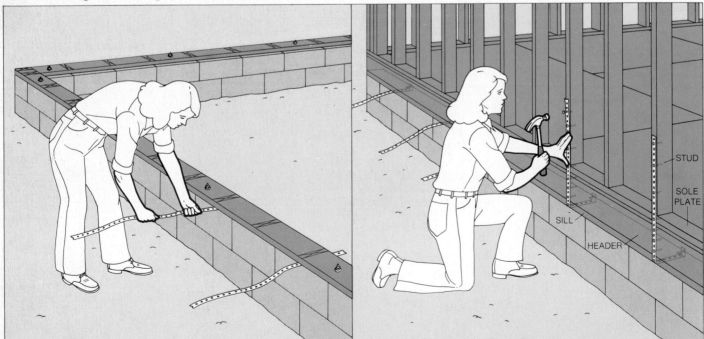

1 **Anchoring foundation, floor and walls.** Slip 30-inch lengths of strapping between the foundation and the loosely bolted sills at every other stud location, pushing through just enough strapping to fold over the inside edge of a sill (above, left). Tighten the sill bolts firmly and nail the strapping to the inner edge of the sill.

When you have installed framing for the floors and walls, nail each length of strapping to the outer faces of the sills, header joists, sole plates and the edges of the studs (above, right). If the sills are set slightly back on the foundation wall to allow space for sheathing flush with the wall, nail the strapping over the sheathing.

2 **Bracing the wall.** From each upper corner of the framed wall, run a metal brace downward at a 45° angle from the top plate to the sole plate; nail the brace to the top plate and sole plate and to each stud that it crosses.

3 **Strapping the roof to the wall.** Shape 36-inch lengths of strapping over the top of every other rafter and over the edges of the top plates and studs below, and nail the strapping to all three members. Follow the same procedure to strengthen the trusses of a truss roof. If rafters or trusses end in an overhang, anchor them with steel-plate connectors (*inset*).

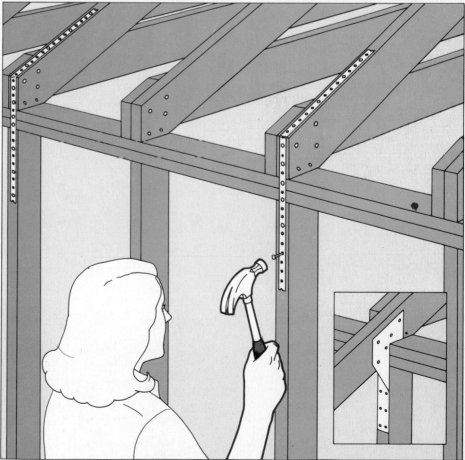

Reinforcing an Existing Structure

Anchoring floors and walls. At the location of every other stud, set a 24-inch steel plate directly against flat siding, such as plywood, and nail it to the sill, header joist, sole plate and stud. In clapboard or other angled siding, cut through the siding to make a recess for the steel plate, so that the plate lies directly against the sheathing.

Linking a wall and a roof. Inside the house, remove sections of wall and ceiling covering to expose every other joint of a stud, top plate and rafter. Nail the end of a 24-inch length of strapping to the face of each exposed rafter, twist the strapping to lie flat against the inside edge of the top plate, twist it again to lie flat against the side of the stud and nail it in place.

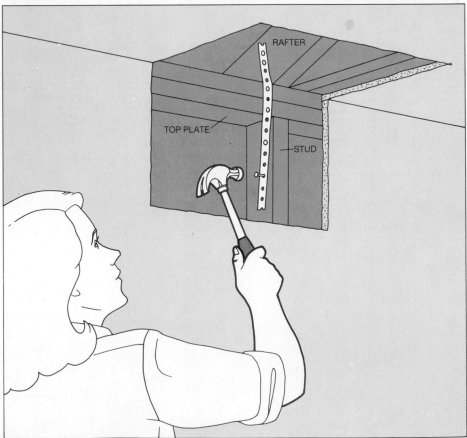

Temporary Ties to Anchor a Cabin

In areas of occasional high winds, you can quickly tie down an unreinforced cabin, employing steel cables and a method used by professional riggers. The only permanent installation is four deadmen—5-foot sections of telephone pole, buried 4 feet deep in trenches parallel to the roof ridge. Each deadman has a 12-foot ¼-inch cable looped and clamped around it and each cable has a turnbuckle on its free end. Where soil is loose or shifting, deadmen must be buried at least 6 feet deep, a job for professionals. If telephone poles are not available for deadmen, you can use railroad ties or pressure-treated 8-by-8s.

You also need to keep ready two steel cables, each long enough to go over the roof from turnbuckle to turnbuckle. The ends of the deadman cables rest on the ground until the Weather Bureau issues a storm warning. Then you run the unattached cables over the roof and attach them to the turnbuckles on the deadman cables. Old tires at the eaves and half-tires placed over the ridge protect the roof when you tighten the turnbuckles. Adjust the turnbuckles only enough to take up slack; too much tension can damage the ridge beam.

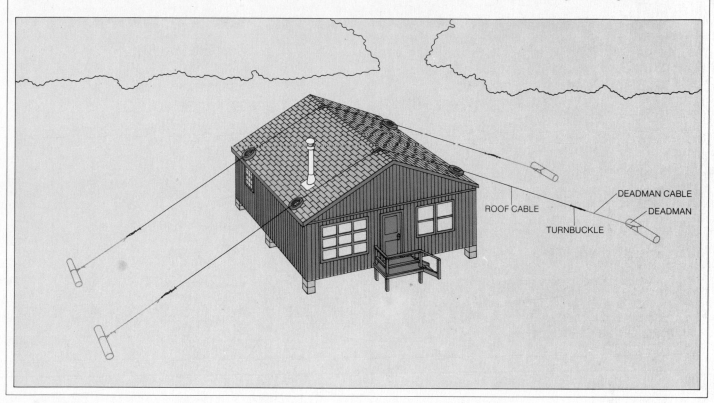

ROOF CABLE

DEADMAN CABLE

DEADMAN

TURNBUCKLE

Strengthening a House in Earthquake Country

Many Americans believe that earthquakes strike California and only California. The fact is that earthquakes occur in many areas of North America *(below)* with enough force to shake an ordinary building to pieces. If you plan to build a vacation retreat in any of these areas, you may wish to reinforce the structure to help it survive a major tremor.

Begin with a strong foundation. One of the strongest is a masonry-block foundation wall *(pages 26-31)*, stiffened with a skeleton of steel reinforcing bars (rebars) and filled with concrete grout. In earthquake country, masons build the wall with masonry blocks called speed blocks *(page 92; and opposite, top)*, especially designed to accommodate vertical and horizontal rebars. Other specially de-

signed blocks permit horizontal rebars to round the corners of the wall without interruption. These lateral stiffeners, embedded in grout in every third or fourth course and in the top course of the foundation wall, are called bond beams.

Strong materials are as important as sound design. Mortar for laying the blocks should be a mixture of 1 part portland cement to 2¼ parts damp, loose sand. In the concrete grout, use sand as the aggregate in a ratio of 3 parts sand to 1 part portland cement. One cubic yard of concrete will make enough grout to fill about 70 blocks.

To reinforce the wall, use No. 5 steel rebar. Vertical bars should be cut long enough to extend 23 inches beyond the top of the footing, then bent to a right

angle 6 inches from one end; the corner bars should have a fairly tight bend to make them fit easily into the corner blocks. Have all of these pieces cut and bent beforehand by a steel fabricator.

A strong foundation alone is not enough to protect a cabin in an earthquake area. Stud walls, for example, should be braced with structural plywood sheathing, fastened to the studs with nails spaced at 6-inch rather than the usual 12-inch intervals.

As a final earthquake-proofing touch, if you have a gas line, have a qualified gas serviceman install an earthquake valve in it *(page 93)*. The valve is designed to shut automatically when shaken by an earthquake, reducing the danger of fire from a ruptured line.

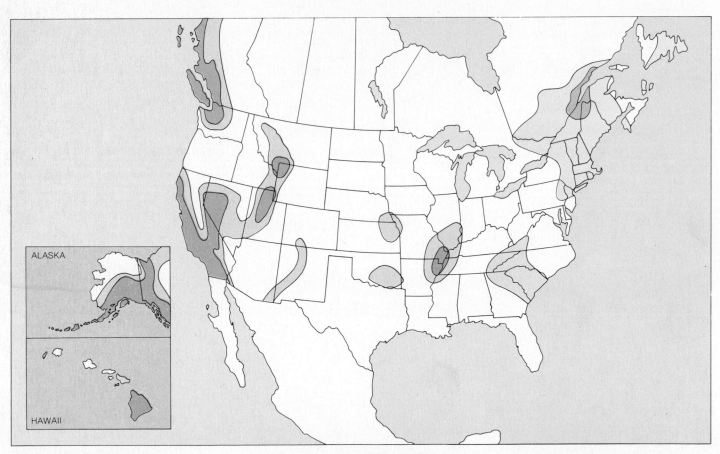

Earthquake areas of North America. In this map of the United States and the most densely populated parts of Canada, dark-red sections represent areas where the risk of severe earthquake is greatest; if you are building in these

areas, the special precautions described on the following pages are advisable. In light-red areas, major earthquakes are less likely but still possible at some locations; in these areas, consult local building officials before you begin

construction to find out whether reinforcement is necessary at your cabin site.

In uncolored areas, earthquakes are rare and few builders construct reinforced dwellings.

Special Blocks for a Strong Foundation

Speed block. These masonry blocks have beveled, open ends that slip sideways around vertical rebars rather than down over them, as conventional blocks would; the single web of each speed block is recessed to accommodate horizontal rebar. Each course of speed block is mortared to the course below and vertically mortared to corner blocks; other vertical joints are not mortared. Concrete grout is added after each course is laid to fill the triangular spaces between the beveled ends of the blocks.

Preparing a bond-beam corner block. A pre-scored block (*near right*) is designed for easy removal of webs and sides to make a path for a horizontal rebar. With light taps of a hammer, knock out the scored section on one side of the block—the side you choose will depend on the direction the block will face when built into the foundation—then knock out both webs.

If prescored blocks are unavailable, make your own bond-beam corner block out of an ordinary two-core corner block (*far right*). With a brickset and a ball-peen hammer, chisel notches 4 inches wide and 3 inches deep as needed into the webs and side of the block.

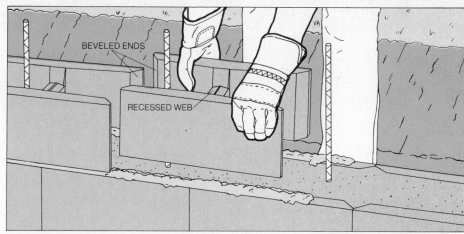

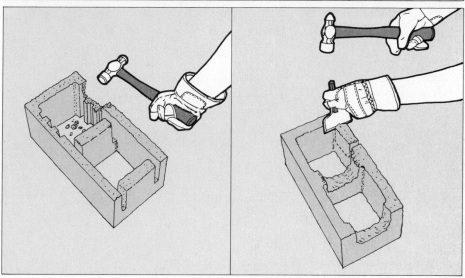

Reinforcing a Foundation Wall

1 Supporting the vertical rebars. Wire prebent vertical reinforcing bars to one line of the horizontal bars laid out for the foundation footing (*page 28*) and to additional stubs driven 2 feet into the ground. Drive two bar stubs at each corner, using the core of a corner block set temporarily into the trench as a guide. Set the remaining stubs 16 inches apart and directly below a string tied between batter boards (*page 27*) to mark the center of the block wall. When all the bars are wired in place, pour the footing.

2 **Grouting the wall.** Build corner leads (page 28, Step 1), using bond-beam corner blocks in the course that will be reinforced with horizontal reinforcing bars, lay the first course of speed blocks (page 91, top) on all four sides of the foundation, and pour concrete grout into the hollows of the first course and down into the first course of the leads. As you pour the grout, have a helper stir it with a stick so that it fills the holes completely, leaving no air pockets. Trowel the grout flush with the tops of the blocks. Lay and grout the second course in the same way. Do not grout the third course (or, if the wall consists of four courses, the fourth) until you have completed Step 3.

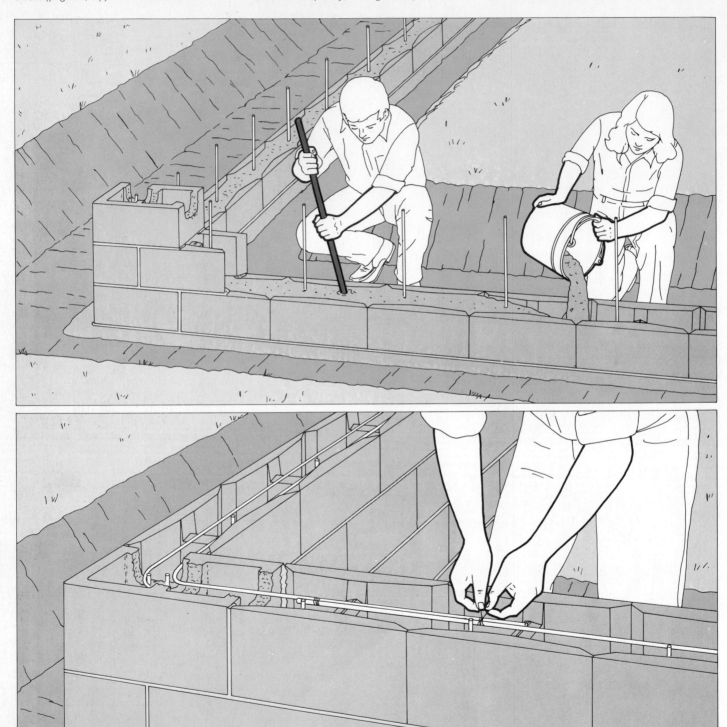

3 **Making a bond beam.** In the channel within the top course of blocks, lay two reinforcing bars, parallel to each other and 2 inches apart, completely around the foundation. At joints between bars, overlap the bars 20 inches and wire them together. At corners, use bars prebent by the supplier to pass through the notches in the webs and side of each bond-beam corner block. Grout the bond beam and embed anchor bolts in the grout (page 29, Step 5).

Stiffening a Frame Wall

Nailing plywood. Before applying whatever exterior covering you plan, sheathe the wall with full and partial panels of ⅜-inch Structural 1 C-D plywood, covering the joists at the top and bottom. Wherever two panels meet without a stud behind the joint, nail 2-by-4 horizontal blocking between studs to support the edges of the panels. Space eightpenny nails 6 inches apart along the edges of all panels; within a panel, space the nails 12 inches apart.

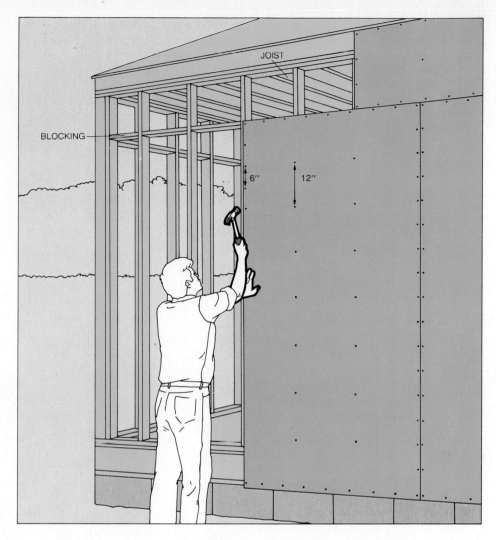

An Array of Earthquake Valves

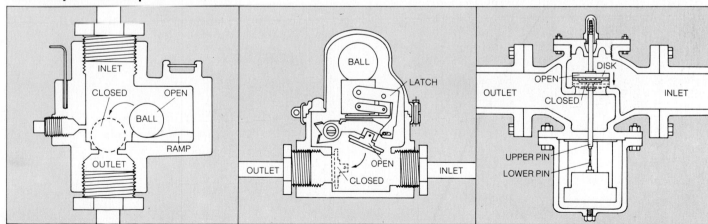

Types of earthquake valves. Designed for professional installation, earthquake valves come in a wide range of designs and prices. Simplest and least expensive is the valve at left, which consists of a metal ball perched on a ramp. When the valve is jolted by a tremor, the ball rolls off the ramp and into the gas line, stopping the flow of gas. In the more sensitive valve at center, a metal ball triggers a latch mechanism that clamps against the outlet end of the valve like a closing door. Most sophisticated is the valve at right, which bears the seal of approval of Underwriters' Laboratories, the fire-protection organization whose recommendation is most widely accepted by fire-fighting agencies and insurance companies. In this valve, a pendulum-weighted lower pin supports an upper pin set into a disk. When an earthquake strikes, the pendulum holds the lower pin stationary; the upper pin, dislodged by the tremor, falls downward and the disk plugs the valve seat.

The Lay of the Land: Clues to Foil a Flood

Water can be a threat to a country cabin. Rushing in a torrent or trickling down a slope, rolling in ocean waves or rising from a flooded river, it can damage or destroy the sturdiest structure. To some extent you can meet the danger by using a special method of construction—building a cabin on a set of high poles, for example, may raise the structure above flood levels—but the real key to protecting a cabin from floods is the right choice of a building site.

Sometimes the choice is fairly obvious: anyone can see that the closer a beach cabin is to the ocean, the more likely it is to be swamped by exceptionally high tides or storm-driven waves. Elsewhere, the problems of correct siting are relatively subtle, and locations that seem ideal at first glance may turn out to be the most vulnerable. A site next to a peaceful stream at the bottom of a ravine or valley, for example, may look safe, especially if you set your cabin well above the water level. Actually, it is a site to be avoided: during or after a heavy rain, the stream is likely to rise rapidly and flow with great force, destroying any property in its path. Other danger spots are shown in the drawings opposite.

Surveyors and landscape architects can identify potential flood problems for you, but you can do a good deal of preliminary detective work yourself before you go to the expense of hiring an expert. To begin with, ask the people of the locality and the area office of the Soil Conservation Service about the history of flooding at or near the site you are considering. Then study the site itself during a rainstorm. As the water runs off, you will see it flowing or collecting in natural drainage paths—areas that should not be blocked by any structure you build.

Vegetation and topographic features give additional clues to potential problems. Plants growing in a generally arid plot of ground indicate a spot that may become a short-lived pond or waterway during a heavy rain. Smooth, rounded boulders were probably shaped by water flowing over them repeatedly in the past. Level ground near creeks and streams is a likely sign of periodic flooding.

If you plan to build at the beach, consult a coastline survey map, available from local building officials. These maps indicate many of the high-hazard areas where wind and waves are likely to cause significant damage to nearby buildings.

A steep ravine or valley. The cabin in the background is sited much too close to a stream running along the bottom of a narrow ravine. In a storm, the volume and velocity of the stream will increase and water will rise up the sides of the steep slope. The cabin at left, situated on a gradual slope well away from the stream, is safe from such flash floods.

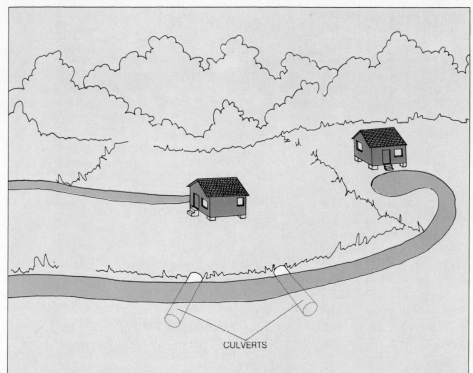

An upland meadow. The cabin at left is located in a depressed area that collects rain water, and the driveway that links it to a main road cuts across the natural drainage path around the building site; in a storm, this roadway would channel water directly into the dishlike meadow. The cabin at right is built on a higher site, which drains quickly; its driveway follows the contour of the land, and underground culverts protect the driveway from a washout.

CULVERTS

Near a river. The cabin in the foreground is built in the oxbow of a river, at the heart of a flood plain; in a heavy rain, the river might widen, completely submerging the site. The cabin in the distance, on a gentle slope well above the flood plain, lies clear of the probable flood pattern.

An ocean beach. The cabin at left, close to the ocean shoreline, is vulnerable to high waves and shifting sands. Even a location farther from the water, on the ocean side of the sand dunes in the middle distance, would be unwise, because it could disturb the natural shifting of sand that forms the protective barrier of dunes. The cabin to the right is located correctly—well behind the first row of dunes and vegetation that form a natural barrier to the waves.

Preparing for the Problems of Deep Snow

Many vacationers dream of an ideal winter retreat—an isolated cabin in a snow-covered landscape. If you share the dream and plan to build your own cabin in snow country, you must meet several mundane requirements to ensure that your dream cottage will remain both usable and comfortable throughout a long, severe winter.

To begin with, you must be able to reach your cabin through deep snow. Do not place a building far from a plowed road unless you plan to get to it by snowshoe or with a snowmobile. Site the house carefully. Hilltops tend to be too windy for winter comfort; idyllic-looking sheltered valleys are generally reservoirs of deep snow and cold air. The best location for a cabin is a south-facing slope, which gets light and warmth from the low winter sun. Fortunately, prevailing winter winds in most snowy parts of North America come from the north or northwest, so that setting your main door and windows toward the sun also keeps them on the downwind side.

The foundation of a snow-country cabin must of course rest below the frost line. Continuous masonry-block foundation walls (pages 26-31) are the warmest type of substructure, and you can insulate them from the outside with packed snow. Insulated walls and, if your budget permits, double-glazed insulating glass for windows, are desirable; drapes or shutters inside the windows help to conserve heat and stop drafts after dark. You can both add to comfort and save on fuel costs by shielding the area outside the main entrance of the cabin with an enclosed entryway—a small antechamber (pages 98-99) that keeps cold winds away from the door and can double as a mud room or a woodshed.

The roof of a snow-country cabin may need thick rafters and special bracing to support the snow, or a steep pitch to shed it (opposite, top). A roof steep enough to shed snow has an obvious advantage but it has disadvantages, too. A steep roof requires far more roofing material to cover a given floor area, and much of the high space underneath may be wasted. Furthermore, a steep roof may require metal strapping or fasteners to tie it down against strong winds that would flow over a lower roof (pages 86-89).

To protect your roof from an overload of snow, clear it after heavy snowfalls with a roof rake—a long-handled scraper, available from hardware stores or homemade by nailing and bracing a 2-foot 1-by-6 across the end of a long pole.

A cabin ready for winter's worst. Sited on a south-facing slope with its principal windows and door away from the winter winds and toward the sun, this cabin takes maximum advantage of whatever warmth and shelter nature can offer. Evergreen trees behind and beside the cabin act as windbreaks, but none are close enough to topple onto the roof. Trees have been cleared from the downwind, south side of the cabin to allow the sun to warm it; one deciduous tree remains, blocking little sun in winter but offering shade in summer. Similarly, the cabin's overhanging eaves block the rays of a high, hot summer sun but let in those of a low winter sun.

The eaves are extended at one point to shelter an enclosed entryway and the steps leading up to it. The roof of the cabin is covered with metal panels, which shed snow readily. A supply of firewood is stored on a sheltered part of the deck, in a spot that is convenient to a side door. A raised boardwalk leads from the front steps to the deck and on out to the driveway; the open deck of the boardwalk itself seldom needs to be shoveled, as it is usually blown clear of snow by the wind.

A snow fence prevents blowing snow from drifting onto the cabin's driveway. Snow deposited by an early winter storm has been plowed off the driveway and pushed as far back as possible, to make space for banks of snow that will be plowed after later storms.

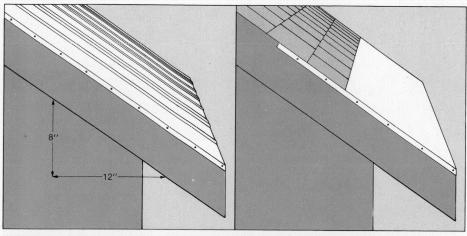

A roof for heavy snows. The slope of the roof at far left—that is, the rate at which it rises, expressed both as an angle and in inches of vertical rise for every 12 inches of horizontal run—is a steep 34°, or 8 inches in 12, a prudent choice for snow country. If this roof is covered with metal panels (*pages 74-75*), it will shed snow. A roof of the same slope, covered with asphalt shingles (*near left*), will hold some snow and needs flashing to keep melting snow from leaking through. The flashing should extend 8 to 10 inches above the line of the walls and lap under the two lowest courses of shingles.

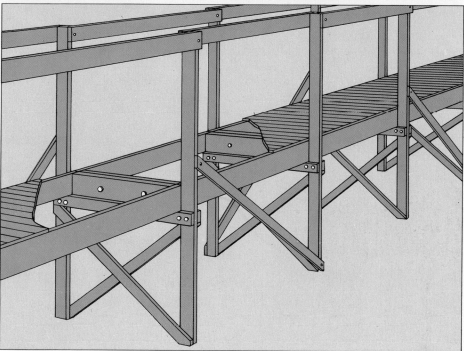

A clear path over snow and mud. The sections of this raised boardwalk can be separated and stored when the ground dries in spring, then reassembled before the first heavy snow. For the walkway sections, make open boxes of 2-by-6s, each 6 feet long and 3 feet wide, with the long boards nailed to the ends of the short ones. Cover the tops of the boxes with 1-by-6 planking, spaced ¼ inch apart for drainage. For each H-shaped support, use 6-foot 2-by-4 uprights 3 feet apart, with a pair of 2-by-4 crosspieces bolted between them 2½ feet from the bottom. Nail diagonal 1-by-4 braces across the bottom half of the H.

To assemble the boardwalk, bolt walkway sections together between the uprights, resting their bottoms on the crosspieces. Bolt 2-by-4 handrails to the tops of the uprights and 1-by-4 diagonal braces from one H to the next. Attach one end of the boardwalk to the cabin and install a flight of steps or build a ramp at the other end.

A Chart of Rafter Sizes

Slope	4″ in 12″			7″ in 12″			10″ in 12″			14″ in 12″			21″ in 12″		
Span	9′	12′	15′	9′	12′	15′	9′	12′	15′	9′	12′	15′	9′	12′	15′
Snow Load															
50 lbs.	2×6	2×8	2×10	2×6	2×8	2×10	2×6	2×8	2×10	2×6	2×8	2×8	2×6	2×6	2×8
60 lbs.	2×6	2×10	2×10	2×6	2×8	2×10	2×6	2×8	2×10	2×6	2×8	2×8	2×6	2×6	2×8
70 lbs.	2×8	2×10	2×12	2×6	2×10	2×10	2×6	2×8	2×10	2×6	2×8	2×10	2×6	2×6	2×8

Picking the right rafters. The chart above gives the correct lumber sizes for rafters in snow regions. The five main vertical columns list common roof slopes in inches per foot (for example, 7 inches of rise in each 12 inches of run); each of these columns is subdivided for rafter spans of 9, 12 and 15 feet (assuming 16-inch spacing). The horizontal rows list ground-snow loads—the expected maximum weights of accumulated snow on flat surfaces—in pounds per square foot. You can get this figure for your area from the local office of the Federal Housing Administration or from a local architect or structural engineer.

To use the chart, first find the vertical column for your roof slope and rafter span, then read down that column to the horizontal row for the snow load in your area. If the exact slope, span and load for your cabin do not appear on the chart, use the next lower figure for slope, the next higher for span and load.

A Doorway Sheltered from Snow and Wind

1 Extending the rafters. To roof an enclosed entryway and the steps leading up to it, extend several rafters of the main roof. Set a 2-by-6 alongside one of these rafters, with its end against the house wall and its top aligned with the top of the rafter; use a level to draw a vertical line on the 2-by-6 at the point where you plan to build the outside wall of the entryway. Take the 2-by-6 down and, using a framing square, draw a line 3½ inches long, running at a right angle from the first line to the bottom edge of the 2-by-6 (*inset*). Cut the board at the lines and use it as a template to cut a 2-by-6 for each of the rafters you will extend. Nail on the two extensions at opposite ends of the entryway.

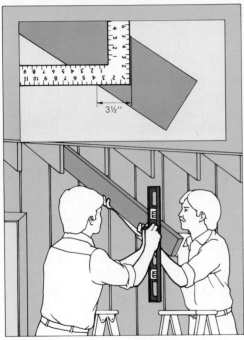

2 Bracing the extended rafters. Brace the end extensions temporarily with horizontal struts nailed to them and resting against the cabin wall. If necessary, use shims between the wall and the ends of the struts to adjust the alignment of the extensions. Hang a plumb bob from the ends of the extensions to locate foundation piers for the entryway. Pour the footings of the piers at the same depth as the footings of the cabin and install two wooden or masonry piers (*pages 14-21*) spanned by a girder of tripled 2-by-8s or 2-by-10s (*page 30*).

3 Hanging the joists. Under the door of the cabin, fasten a 2-by-8 joist plate to the wall with its bottom edge level with the top of the entryway girder; use ⅜-inch lag bolts 5 inches long, screwed through siding and sheathing into the header joist or end joist of the cabin (if necessary, remove a section of siding to fit the plate flat against the wall). Drop a plumb bob from the extended rafters to mark the girder and the plate for joists and, at the marks, nail joist hangers to the plate and anchors to the girder. Fasten 2-by-8 joists to the hangers and anchors.

Cover the joists with ¾-inch exterior-grade plywood for a solid floor, or with decking of 2-by-6s separated by ¼-inch spaces. Fasten steps to hangers on the end joist, resting the bottom of the steps on a shallow concrete footing.

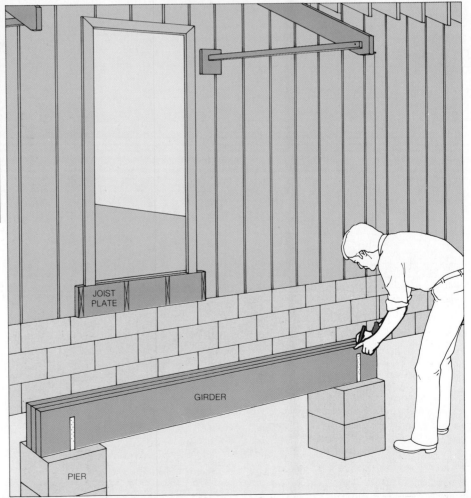

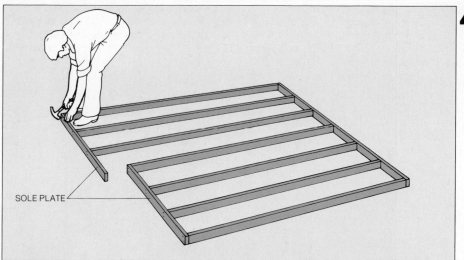

SOLE PLATE

4 **Framing the outside wall.** Assemble a frame of studs and plates on the ground. First cut 2-by-4 top and sole plates to the length of the outside wall and mark them for studs at the rafter spacing. Because part of the sole plate will rest on the entryway floor and part on the slightly lower girder, the studs above it must be of unequal lengths. Cut the plate in two at the point where the floor ends; cut the studs to fit between the top plate and the two sections of sole plate.

With a helper, lift the wall frame into position. Nail the sole plate to the girder and through the entryway floor into the joists. Toenail the end rafters to the top plate, remove the struts and install the remaining rafters.

5 **Framing the end walls.** Nail sole plates to the floor at the ends of the entryway and cut studs to fit beneath the sloping rafters, notching them as illustrated (*inset*). Frame the door by the method shown on pages 37 and 39.

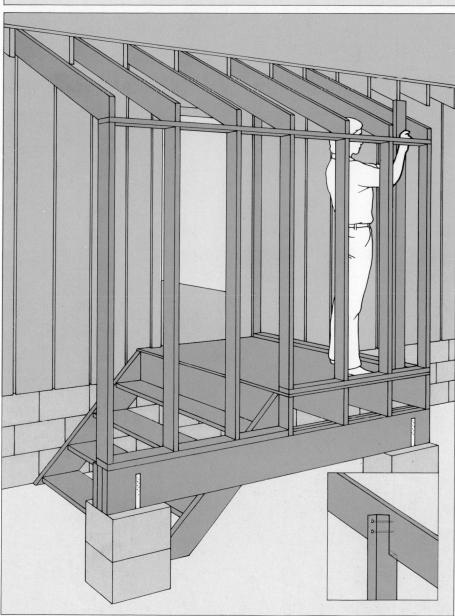

4 Adding the Amenities

Parts for a driven well. The perforated, spear-like drive point at center can be hammered down through sandy soil to water that lies as much as 30 feet below the surface. Sections of metal pipe are coupled to the shaft of the drive point until the water is tapped, then a flexible plastic pipe is fitted to the top section with a plastic pipe adapter (*bottom*) and routed to the cabin. An old-fashioned pitcher pump (*top*) draws the water through the metal and plastic pipes to a countertop in the cabin kitchen.

Just because you are getting away from it all does not mean that you must give up any kind of basic comfort, even when your cabin or cottage is not equipped with conveniences that you take for granted at home—electricity, central heating or an endless supply of hot and cold running water. Until fairly recently, most people got along quite nicely without these conveniences. Many old-fashioned ways can be readily adapted to a comfortable vacation retreat, and you will soon discover that most modern necessities are not quite so necessary to comfort as you may have thought—at least for a few days at a time.

For light and cooking, the kerosene, propane or gasoline lamps and stoves developed for campers serve admirably inside a cabin. And without such luxury appliances as a dishwasher or washing machine, water-supply requirements will be relatively slight. You may be able simply to tap an adjacent stream or pond, or use a cistern to collect rain water. In most cases, however, some sort of well is necessary; generally it is best drilled or dug by a professional, but a pump is fairly easy to install yourself.

There are a number of ways to bring water into your cabin. A small, hand-operated pump mounted on a counter next to a kitchen sink is not only picturesque but practical. If you prefer a more convenient source of running water and are using an electrically powered pump, you can install a pressurized tank that will force water under pressure to a conventional faucet.

You may not have access to a sewer line for waste-water disposal, but for the limited amounts of water that you will be using, you will not need an elaborate waste-treatment system. In most localities, you can pipe your waste water to a simple seepage pit or to a small drainage field where the water is absorbed into the ground.

A flush toilet may be the convenience you will miss the most. But a well-constructed privy—the type that once was a fixture outside nearly every American home—can be a comfortable enough alternative, especially if it is used primarily during mild weather. For the colder months, you may want to consider a chemical toilet that can be installed indoors.

A wood-burning stove will throw out enough heat to keep a cabin snugly warm even in sub-zero weather, and if you clear away a number of trees on your building site, you will have a ready-made source of fuel. Otherwise, wood-gathering is permitted at many state and national forests, and it does not take long to lay in a season's supply. As for keeping food cold for storage, you can have a gas-powered refrigerator as efficient as the sleek electrical model of your year-round house; use tanks of propane gas to run the refrigerator, but have a professional install the gas line.

Water: From Where It Is to Where You Need It

One of the most taken-for-granted conveniences of modern life is water—a stream of fresh water at the twist of a tap. Bringing such a stream to a cabin may simply involve connecting up to a public water line. If you are off the beaten path, far from public utilities, you can generally tap a supply of surface water, rain water or ground water. (Before you do so, have the water checked for contaminants by the state health department.)

Surface water from a stream or lake is the easiest to tap. If the water is uphill from your site, fit plastic pipe with an intake—a cone of screening—drop the pipe in the water and run it to a tap. If the water is downhill, attach a pump—hand- or power-operated—to the pipe.

Rain water can be collected almost as easily as surface water by a catchment system (opposite, bottom) in which water runs off a roof into screened gutters, down a drainspout, and into a roof washer, a contraption consisting of a screened trough leading into a plastic garbage can. Plastic pipe carries water from the can down to a holding tank, or cistern (page 104), to be pumped out as needed.

A 275-gallon cistern—which is sold as a galvanized-steel pressure tank by plumbing suppliers—holds enough water for weekend use by a family of six. To purify cistern water, add ¼ cup of liquid chlorine laundry bleach for each 300 gallons of water after every rainfall. Drain the cistern annually and flush out sediment with fresh water.

Where surface and rain water are not readily utilized, well water almost always is. At a site on a sandy soil, you may be able to tap it easily. Check with neighbors; if their experience indicates that ground water in the area generally is within 30 feet of the surface, you can drive a well by hammering a pipe down. In a soil so dense or rocky that you cannot drive a pipe, you can turn to an old-fashioned dug well. Once laboriously excavated by pick and shovel, such wells are now easily dug by a backhoe. A ceramic casing protects the shaft from cave-ins; water that collects at the bottom is pumped like surface water.

Where water is not within 30 feet of the surface, most people turn to a professional, whose equipment can drill as deep as necessary to reach water. A professional will also install and seal a galvanized-steel casing. From that point, you can lower an electric pump into the well (page 112) and hook it up.

The piping for any of these systems is easily done with 1- and 1¼-inch flexible polyethylene plastic pipe and hard plastic fittings widely available from building-supply dealers. You can connect pipe to the metal, female-threaded openings on pumps, tanks or well casings with a flexible pipe adapter—a plastic fitting with a male thread at one end and a ridged neck at the other. The male end of the adapter is threaded into the female-threaded opening of the pump or other device and the ridged neck is inserted into the pipe and secured with a stainless-steel hose clamp. If a female thread is larger than 1 or 1¼ inches, you may need an adapter plus a reducer bushing—a ring threaded on the inside and outside, with outside dimensions that match the female threads on the device and an inside diameter that matches the pipe adapter. Always cover male threads with pipe-joint tape or compound.

An Intake for Surface Water

1 **Assembling the intake-pipe fittings.** Using as much 1-inch flexible-plastic pipe as you need to reach your downhill tap or uphill pump, insert into its intake end the ridged end of a 1-inch pipe adapter, used to connect female threads to this piping, and secure the pipe with a hose clamp. Wrap pipe-joint tape around the threads of the adapter, beginning at the outer end and following the direction of the threads, and screw on a 1-inch intake screen.

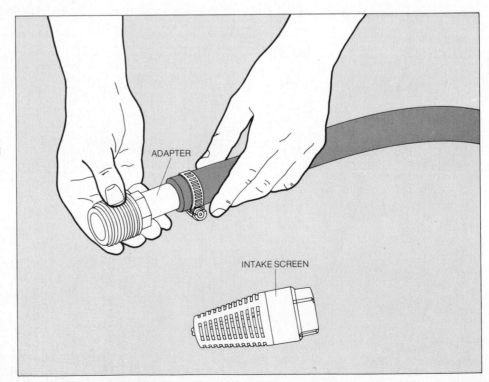

ADAPTER

INTAKE SCREEN

2 **Positioning the pipe in the water.** Run the intake end of the pipe through the core of a masonry block, tie a length of nylon cord to the intake screen and place the block on the river or lake bottom as far from shore as you can safely wade. Tie the other end of the cord to a float—a stoppered jug—to hold the intake at least 2 feet above the bottom. Hook up the free end of the pipe to a tap if the cabin is downhill, to a pump (*pages 107-108*) if the cabin is uphill.

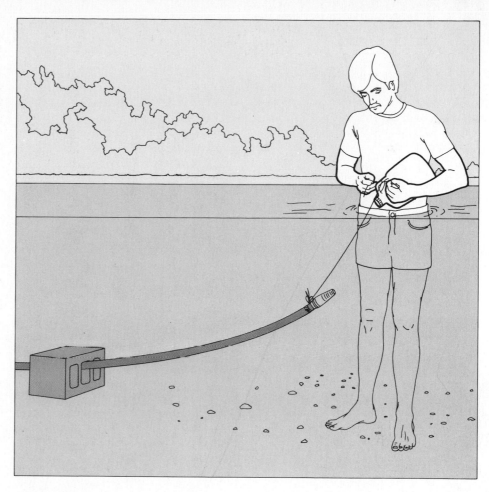

A Catchment for Rain Water

1 **Connecting the pipe.** Cut a 1¾-inch-diameter opening 10 inches from the top of a new 30-gallon plastic garbage can and insert the plastic sink connection called a 1½-inch PVC drain adapter, securing it with its nut. To connect the unthreaded outer end of this adapter to your 1-inch plastic pipe, assemble the parts illustrated in the inset, first cementing to the sink adapter a 1½-inch female-threaded adapter, then screwing on a 1½-inch-to-1¼-inch reducer bushing and a 1¼-inch male adapter, and finally attaching with a hose clamp enough 1¼-inch plastic pipe to reach the cistern.

Drill a ⅛-inch hole 2 inches from the bottom of the can as a drain, so that the can will not remain full of water between rains.

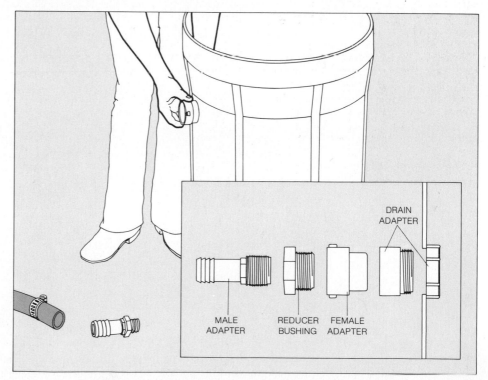

MALE ADAPTER   REDUCER BUSHING   FEMALE ADAPTER   DRAIN ADAPTER

2 **Assembling the roof washer.** Make a trough to break the force of water from the roof by nailing 1-by-4 sides to a plywood square having a 4-inch hole in its center; staple ¼-inch galvanized screening over the top.

Install a roof gutter (or clean an existing one) and add a downspout (or shorten an existing one) to empty about 6 inches above your plastic can. Shield the gutter with 5-foot lengths of the plastic screening sold as gutter guard (*inset*), cutting and bending them so that they fit snugly at sides and ends and around braces.

TROUGH BOTTOM

3 **Connecting the cistern.** Place the cistern—buy what is called a galvanized-steel pressure tank in the size you need—as close to the cabin as possible but with its top below the level of the roof-washer outlet. If necessary, raise the washer on a platform or dig a pit for the cistern.

Connect the pipe from the roof washer to the 1¼-inch threaded opening near the bottom of the cistern with a 1¼-inch pipe adapter. Remove the threaded plug on top of the tank, replace it with a nipple—a 6-inch length of 1½-inch pipe with male threads at each end—and screw on a 1½-inch vent cap, a mushroom-shaped fitting with holes to let air out of the tank as it fills.

Insert a 1¼-to-1-inch threaded reducer bushing into the opening near the bottom of the tank opposite the intake from the roof washer and run another pipe inside your home to a hand or jet pump (*pages 106-108*)—the two kinds suitable for use with a cistern.

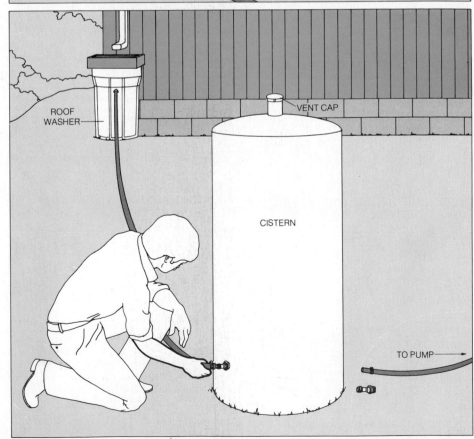

ROOF WASHER

VENT CAP

CISTERN

TO PUMP

Driving Your Own Well

1 Attaching a drive-point shaft. Join the drive-point shaft—a special section of galvanized steel pipe with screened openings and a sharp point at one end—to a 4-foot section of 1¼-inch galvanized steel pipe with a coupling, a short length of pipe internally threaded at both ends. Secure the pipes by using two pipe wrenches. Screw to the other end of the pipe a drive cap, a closure that covers and protects the pipe threads, and push the drive point into a pilot hole 2 feet deep.

2 Hammering pipe sections. With a sledge hammer, drive the assembly a foot into the ground, then retighten the coupling around the pipe and drive point. Tap the assembly sideways for the first few feet to keep it fairly plumb. When you have driven the top of the assembly almost down to ground level, remove the drive cap, add another section of pipe with a coupling, as in Step 1, and put the drive cap on it. Drive the assembly another foot into the ground and retighten the coupling as before.

Each time you remove the drive cap to add sections of pipe, lower a string with a nut tied to the end inside the piping. When you hear a splash from the bottom of the shaft, you have reached water; drive the piping 2 feet deeper.

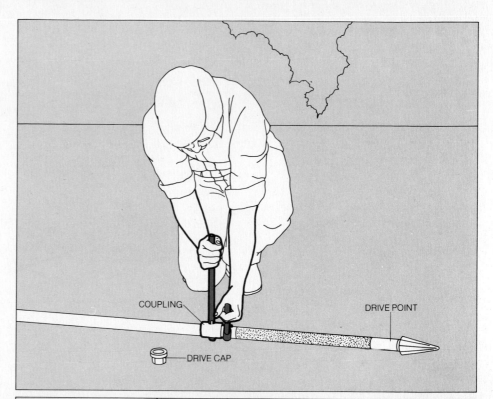

COUPLING DRIVE POINT

DRIVE CAP

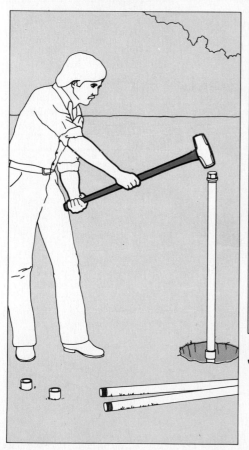

3 Capping the well pipe. Remove the drive cap and thread a metal 1¼-inch T fitting with a 1-inch side outlet to the pipe. Tighten the fitting with a pipe wrench and plug the top of the T with a 1¼-inch threaded plug.

Thread a 1-inch plastic pipe adapter to the side outlet, clamp flexible plastic pipe to it and run the pipe to your pump. If the flow of water is insufficient when you use the pump, the drive-point screen may be clogged. To clear it, use the pump briefly and remove the plug from the top of the T fitting—the water will fall back down the well pipe and force sand and sediment away from the screen. Repeat this procedure until water flows freely.

Picking the Right Pump

Depending on the source of water and the power available, your choice of pumps ranges from an old-fashioned pitcher, or lift, pump and the equally venerable wind-powered pump to modern electric jet and submersible models.

The least expensive, most easily installed pump is the pitcher pump, consisting of an iron cylinder fitted with a leather-rimmed piston, a handle to move the piston, and a pipe running from the cylinder to the water supply. A pitcher pump works only if the water level is less than 25 feet lower than the pump.

Among the power-operated pumps, which raise water any distance necessary,

the one most often used with surface sources is the jet pump *(right)*, which pulls the water to a pressure tank. The power pump most popular for deep drilled wells is the submersible type *(page 109)*, which pushes water up to the tank. If you cannot plug into utility power at or near your building site, you will need a generator—4,000 watts or more—to power a jet or submersible pump.

If you do not plan to use your cabin in winter, open all of the valves and draincocks in your water system—disassembling pipes if necessary—to let water out and air into parts of the system that will be exposed to freezing temperatures.

Installing a Lift Pump

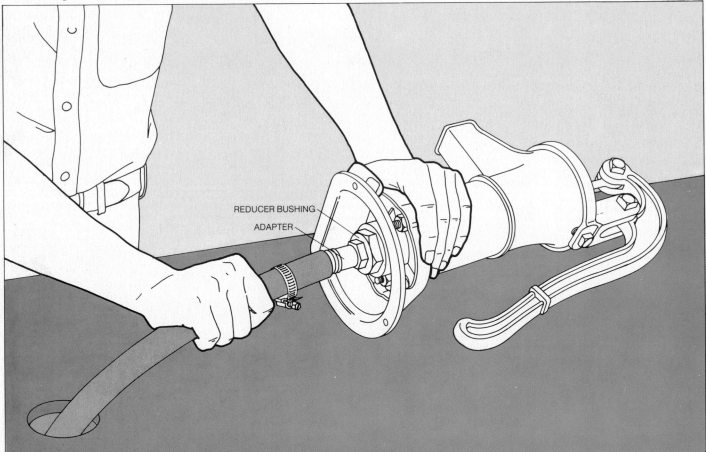

REDUCER BUSHING

ADAPTER

Mounting the pump indoors. Run 1-inch flexible pipe from your source of water up through a 2-inch hole cut in the counter next to your sink. Thread a 1¼-to-1-inch reducer bushing into the 1¼-inch fitting in the bottom of the pump and join the pipe to the bushing with a 1-inch male

pipe adapter and hose clamp. Screw the pump to the countertop.

Before you work the pump handle to draw water up, pour a cup of water into the top of the pump to wet the leather seals inside.

Installing a Jet Pump

A jet-pump layout. The installation below, capable of raising water more than 25 feet, consists of two major parts: an electric pump in a sheltered location at a cabin; and an ejector unit near a source of surface water. (Simpler models, designed to raise water less than 25 feet, house both components in a single installation at a cabin.) The pump draws water up a 1-inch intake pipe, through the ejector, and up a 1¼-inch suction pipe. Part of the water returns to the ejector unit through a 1-inch pressure pipe; inside the unit, this jet of water squirts through a nozzle, expands in a flared tube, and creates a partial vacuum that can help suck water to the pump from depths as great as 120 feet.

At the pump, the water that is not returned to the ejector flows through an outlet pipe to a pressure tank (*page 108*), from which it is drawn for use in the cabin. As the tank empties, its pressure drops; eventually, when the pressure falls to a predetermined point, a pressure switch mounted on the pump closes to run the pump until pressure is restored. During periods when the pump is not running, a check valve located between the intake and the ejector unit closes to keep water trapped in the system.

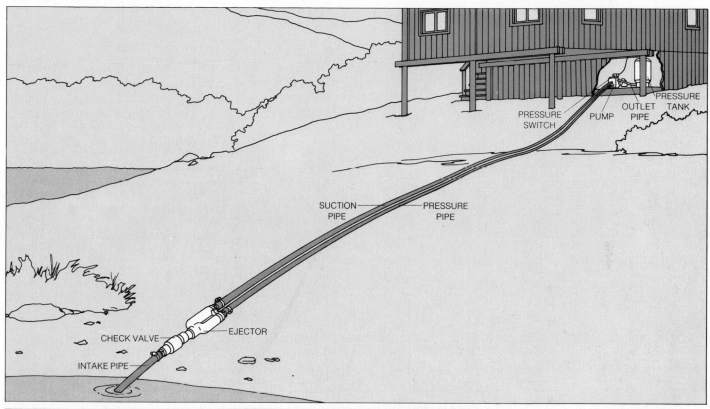

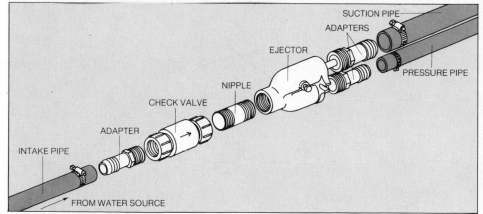

Connections at the ejector. Start the assembly by screwing a nipple—a short piece of 1-inch pipe, threaded at both ends—into the single-ended intake of the ejector; then screw the check valve onto the nipple, with the flow-direction arrow of the valve pointing toward the ejector.

Screw a flexible pipe adapter into the other end of the check valve, insert the adapter into the intake pipe and fasten it there with a hose clamp. At the double-ended openings of the ejector, use adapters and clamps in the same way to hook up the suction and pressure pipes.

Connections at the pump. Using flexible pipe adapters and hose clamps, join the pressure and suction pipes to the matching openings on the pump. Attach ¾-inch plastic pipe to the pump outlet with a ¾-inch adapter and a clamp, and run this pipe to the pressure tank.

Connections at the pressure tank. Begin these connections by screwing a special four-arm T assembly, available from the pressure-tank dealer, into the threaded opening at the base of the tank. Screw a standard T fitting onto one side of the assembly; and screw a drain valve, used to empty the tank whenever necessary, into the middle of this fitting. At the remaining opening, install a 1-inch nipple and a gate valve, which controls the flow of water to the cabin. Into the middle arm of the four-arm T, screw a pressure-relief valve, which automatically bleeds excess pressure from the tank.

To link the tank with a jet pump, seal the two small openings at the top of the four-arm T with pipe plugs, and fit the remaining opening with a 1-inch coupling and a 1-to-¾-inch reducer bushing. Connect the bushing to the pump line with a flexible pipe adapter and a hose clamp.

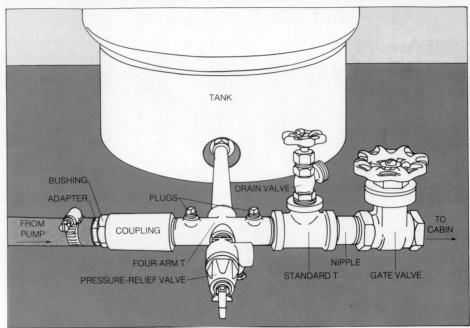

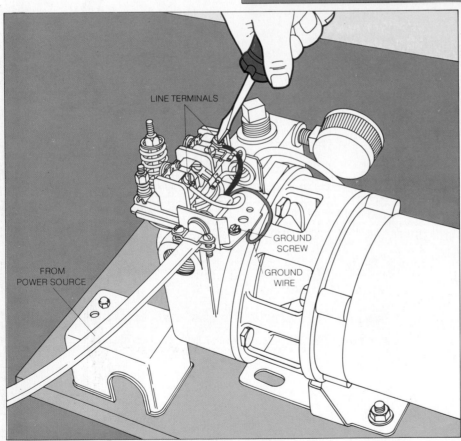

Wiring a pressure switch. For a jet pump, run 14-gauge cable from a power source to the terminals of the pressure switch, and screw the power wires (black and white in a 120-volt cable, black and either white or red in a 240-volt cable) to the outside switch terminals, which are marked "line." Attach the bare or green ground wire to the grounding screw.

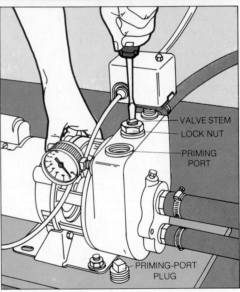

Priming a jet pump. Open the drain valve of the pressure tank, remove the plug from the priming port, then loosen the lock nut and tighten the stem of the control valve, which regulates water pressure. Pour water into the port until the pump is completely full, then wrap the threads of the port plug with pipe-joint tape and screw the plug loosely in place. Turn the pump on. Air bubbles will pop from the priming port; when they stop, tighten the plug and loosen the stem until the needle on the pressure gauge is at the mark specified by the manufacturer—generally 20 to 25 pounds per square inch. Tighten the lock nut and close the drain valve.

On some jet pumps a hexagonal-head bolt regulates the water pressure. To set the control valve in these models, turn the bolt according to the manufacturer's instructions.

A Submersible Pump for a Drilled Well

Developed over 80 years ago for mines and oil wells, the submersible pump has become the type most widely used in private water systems. It is silent, invisible and virtually maintenance-free.

The professional who drills your well and installs its steel casing will recommend the size of pump you need; accessories for the installation are available from pump dealers and plumbing suppliers. If your well is less than 400 feet deep, you can install the pump yourself, by attaching it to flexible plastic pipe (ask the well driller to specify the length and grade of the pipe). In wells that are deeper than 400 feet, the pump must be fitted with heavy sections of galvanized-steel pipe, joined every 20 feet with couplings—a job best left to the professional.

A submersible-pump layout. Hung from a well pipe into the water of a drilled well, this submersible pump has just above it a flexible "torque arrester" that fits tightly against the well casing to keep the well pipe from moving when the pump starts. The pipe itself is attached to an opening in the casing with a fitting called a pitless adapter, which seals the opening around the pipe; from this point, water flows through a supply pipe to a pressure tank.

A pair of waterproof pump wires, threaded through disks called cable guards, runs up from the pump alongside the well pipe. At the top of the casing, these wires run into an electrical junction box, where they are spliced to the wires of UF cable, designed for burial beneath the ground. The UF cable runs down the outside of the casing inside a length of plastic conduit, then goes underground to a pressure switch mounted on the pressure tank.

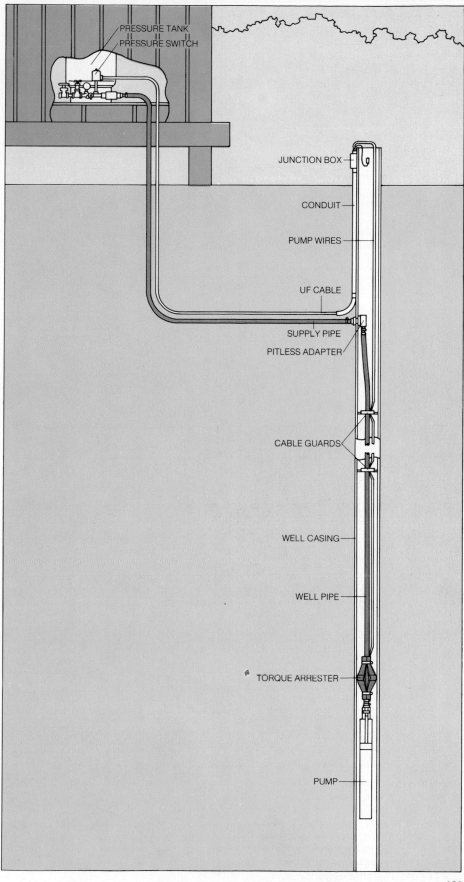

PRESSURE TANK
PRESSURE SWITCH
JUNCTION BOX
CONDUIT
PUMP WIRES
UF CABLE
SUPPLY PIPE
PITLESS ADAPTER
CABLE GUARDS
WELL CASING
WELL PIPE
TORQUE ARRESTER
PUMP

Installing a Submersible Pump

1 Putting in a pitless adapter. Dig a trench just below the frost line from the house to the well casing and, working at the bottom of the trench, install the adapter assembly *(inset)* in the side of the casing. Begin this part of the job by cutting a hole to fit the adapter nipple in the casing, using a hole saw made for cutting steel and a ⅜- or ½-inch electric drill. Slip the inner gasket of the adapter over the threaded nipple, fit the bracket of the nipple onto the slider plate and secure the plate temporarily to a T-shaped handle, assembled from plastic pipe and fittings.

From above, lower the T-shaped handle down the casing until the nipple is at the level of the hole you have cut. Have a helper at the bottom of the trench pull the nipple through the hole and secure it in place with the outer gasket, retainer ring and nut. Pull the slider plate up from the bracket and out of the casing.

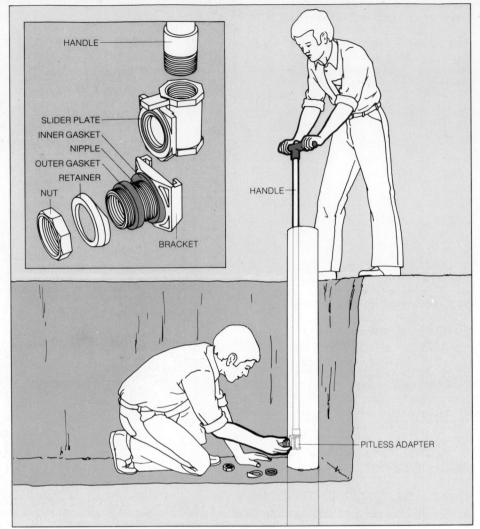

HANDLE

SLIDER PLATE

INNER GASKET

NIPPLE

OUTER GASKET

RETAINER

NUT

BRACKET

HANDLE

PITLESS ADAPTER

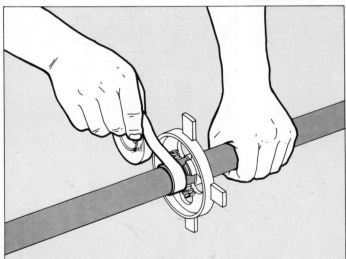

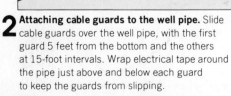

2 Attaching cable guards to the well pipe. Slide cable guards over the well pipe, with the first guard 5 feet from the bottom and the others at 15-foot intervals. Wrap electrical tape around the pipe just above and below each guard to keep the guards from slipping.

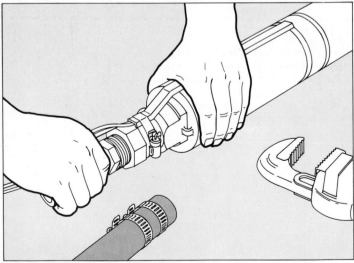

3 Linking the pipe and the pump. Slide a pair of hose clamps over the bottom of the well pipe, and screw a flexible-pipe adapter into the opening at the top of the pump; then tighten the adapter with a pipe wrench. Slip the pipe over the adapter and tighten the clamps.

4 **Linking slider plate to well pipe.** Screw a flexible-pipe adapter to the free end of the slider plate you removed from the pitless adapter (*opposite, Step 1*), and attach the well pipe to the adapter, using two clamps, one behind the other. Grease the rubber gasket in the plate with the lubricant supplied by the manufacturer and seal the opening within the gasket temporarily with tape to keep out dirt.

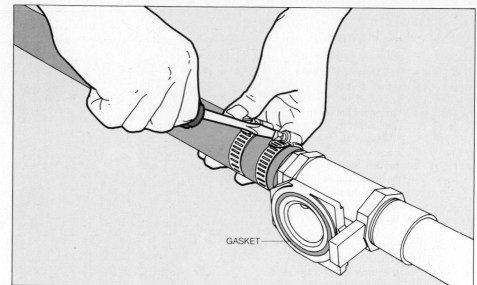

GASKET

5 **Extending the pump wires.** Splice the pump wires to extensions running the full length of the well pipe. Begin this step of the job by threading a pair of submersible-pump wires through the cable guards, leaving 10 feet of slack at the upper end of the pipe. Slide a greased boot—a rubber cylinder used to protect a splice—over one of the pump wires, strip ½ inch of insulation from the ends of the pump and extension wires and splice the two wires in a metal crimp connector with an electrician's multipurpose tool, then slide the boot over the crimp. Splice the other pump and extension wires in the same way and fasten both splices to the pipe with tape.

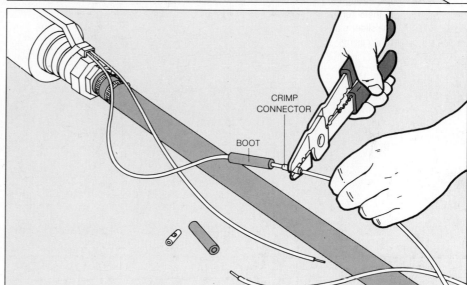

CRIMP CONNECTOR

BOOT

6 **Installing the torque arrester.** Around the well pipe just above the pump, loosely clamp the halves of a rubber torque arrester. Force the ends of the arrester toward each other, expanding the middle until it matches the inside diameter of the well casing. Hold the arrester in this position while a helper tightens the clamps.

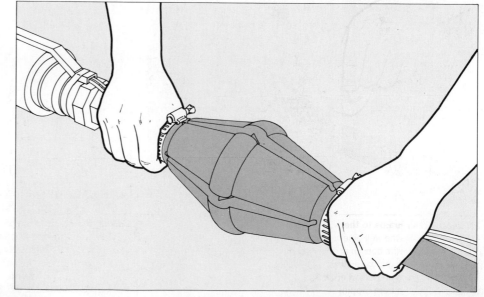

7 Installing the pump and junction box. Pad the edges of the well casing with rags to protect the pump extension wires, then lower the pump into the casing as a helper feeds pipe to you. When your helper comes to the T-shaped handle, untape the opening in the slider plate of the pitless adapter and lower the plate until it slips into the bracket fastened inside the casing (*page 110, Step 1*). Twist the handle to secure the slider plate, then push the handle down firmly and unscrew the handle from the plate. Join 1-inch flexible plastic pipe to the pitless-adapter nipple with a plastic pipe adapter, run the pipe to the pressure tank and attach it, following the procedure used for the jet pump (*page 108*) with two exceptions: substitute a check valve (*page 107*) for the 1-inch coupling, and install a pressure gauge and a pressure switch in the small openings on the T assembly.

8 Assembling the conduit. Assemble a curved plastic conduit section, a straight length of plastic conduit and a plastic fitting called a C body, which serves as an electrical junction box, adjusting the length of the straight section so that the box is just below the top of the well casing and the curved section lies at the bottom of the trench. Run UF cable from the pressure switch along the trench, through the conduit and into the junction box. Push the ends of the pump extension wires down into the box.

Drill a ¼-inch hole 2 inches from the top of the casing near the junction box and use the hole to attach an aluminum grounding block inside the casing with a nut and bolt.

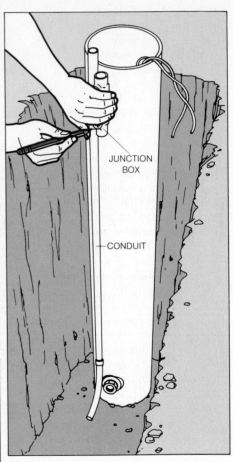

JUNCTION BOX

CONDUIT

9 Connections at the wellhead. Strip 8 inches of plastic sheathing from the UF cable and join its black and white wires to the pump extension wires with wire caps. Run the bare ground wire of the cable through the top of the junction box and over the well casing, and secure it with the setscrew of the grounding block. Install the cover of the junction box and seal the casing with a well cap that fits over both the casing and the junction box.

At the pressure switch, connect the power wires of the underground cables to the inside switch terminals marked "load." Connect the wires from your power source as you would those of a jet pump (*page 108*), but leave the ground wire free. Use a wire cap to join the ground wires of both cables to a short jumper wire, and connect the jumper to the grounding screw.

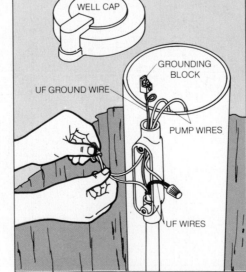

WELL CAP

GROUNDING BLOCK

UF GROUND WIRE

PUMP WIRES

UF WIRES

Pumping Water with Wind Power

Until the 1930s, when electric power lines spread over most rural areas, the towering windmill of a water pump was a familiar sight across the American landscape. Today, as vacationers go farther and farther afield in search of cabin sites, windmills are becoming popular again for the same purpose.

To determine whether a windmill-powered pump is a practical way of bringing water to your cabin, you must first make sure that you have enough wind. A typical windmill such as the one at right requires a wind speed of at least 7 mph to operate. For information about the wind conditions that prevail in your area, call the local weather service station listed in the telephone directory under the U.S. Department of Commerce, Transport Canada or Environment Canada.

If there is enough wind to power a pump, have your well drilled by a professional; then install your own footings or piers (pages 18-21). If you have experience in working at heights, you may want to assemble the windmill itself, which goes together like the parts of a giant Erector set; generally, though, this is a job for professionals.

Most windmills come in a kit that includes a mill assembly and steel tower. The tower should be at least 10 feet taller than any obstructions within a 400-foot radius (in hurricane areas, you may need to install a hinged "Gulf States" tower, which can be tipped down and anchored before a storm). Installed on a platform atop the tower, the mill assembly is composed of a wheel spun by wind-catching sails and mounted on a shaft and a gearbox. A long tail, or vane, keeps the wheel turned into the wind.

Suspended inside the well at the end of a galvanized-steel well pipe is a force-pump cylinder containing a piston and a pump rod. The end of the rod is connected to a pole that runs up the tower gearbox. When the sails catch the wind, the wheel's rotary motion is converted to an up-and-down motion that moves the pump rod and piston, and the pump draws water to an outlet at the top of the well.

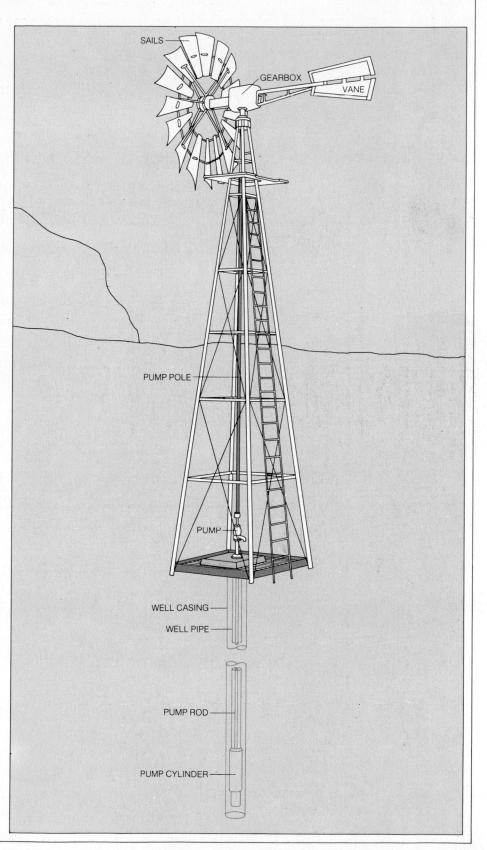

Putting In an All-purpose Sink

A kitchen sink with running water was the first sign of civilized comfort during the settling of the West, and it is the basic amenity for even a Spartan vacation cabin. This minimum of equipment turns cooking, meal cleanups and personal washing into simple indoor routines rather than difficult outdoor chores.

The sink is an easily added convenience if you have any kind of pump-delivered water supply—electric pumps provide the water wherever you want it, and even a hand-operated pitcher pump *(page 106)* can be mounted indoors. The sink easiest to set up is an inexpensive plastic laundry tub, which has the added advantage of large size. However, if your pump is hand-operated, you will need a counter to mount the pump on; in that case, a better choice for a sink is probably the stainless-steel type designed to be attached to a ready-made counter or a plywood shelf.

Flexible plastic pipe brings water in to a pump or faucet. Waste runs out through rigid plastic traps and T fittings into a drain line of flexible pipe leading to a drainage system.

The waste from a sink is what sanitary experts call gray water, since it contains relatively little organic matter. In many rural areas, particularly in Europe, it simply goes into an open channel and eventually seeps into the ground, like rainwater from downspouts. However, gray water will contain such contaminants as soapsuds and food particles. At a minimum, a pit *(page 116)* is advisable for drainage; many codes require a complete septic system *(page 118)*.

The basic sink. In this installation, water from an electric pump comes through plastic pipe to a faucet mounted in one of the holes of a standard kitchen sink; the other holes are capped with faucet-hole covers, available from a plumbing supplier. The sink is mounted in a hole cut through a plywood shelf, with clips provided by the manufacturer. If a hand-operated pump is used, plug all sink holes except for the drain hole at the bottom of the basin and mount the pump on the counter to empty into the sink *(page 106)*. For drainage, fit the sink with a straight tailpiece and a P-shaped trap; from the trap, route the waste to the drainpipe through an elbow, a trap arm and a T fitting. In this installation a special in-house vent, permissible in many areas in place of a through-the-roof vent, is attached to the top of the T.

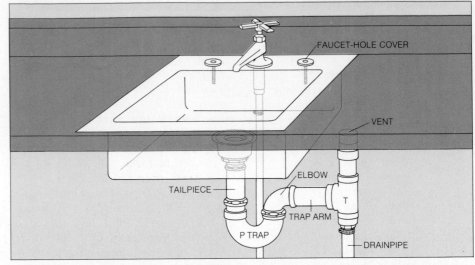

FAUCET-HOLE COVER

VENT

TAILPIECE

ELBOW

T

TRAP ARM

P TRAP

DRAINPIPE

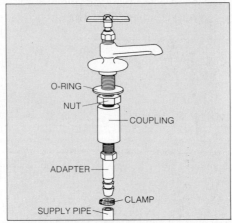

O-RING

NUT

COUPLING

ADAPTER

CLAMP

SUPPLY PIPE

Assembling the supply. Before mounting the sink in the counter, install the faucet and the connections to the supply pipe. Caulk the underside of the faucet base with plumber's putty and attach the faucet in the sink hole with an O-ring and nut; screw on a steel coupling and attach a flexible-pipe adapter to the coupling. Install strainer and tailpiece *(below)*, then mount the sink, slide the supply pipe over the adapter and secure the pipe with a hose clamp.

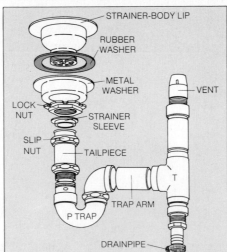

STRAINER-BODY LIP

RUBBER WASHER

METAL WASHER

VENT

LOCK NUT

STRAINER SLEEVE

SLIP NUT

TAILPIECE

T

TRAP ARM

P TRAP

DRAINPIPE

Assembling the drains. Before installing the sink, apply putty to the underside of the strainer-body lip and insert the strainer body into the drain hole. Slip on rubber and metal washers and secure with a lock nut. Then assemble the strainer sleeve, slip nut and tailpiece and connect the tailpiece to the strainer body.

After the sink is mounted, fasten the P trap to the tailpiece with a slip nut and washer. Connect the trap to the T with a short piece of pipe called the trap arm. To the top of the T attach a 4-inch pipe that fits into a female-threaded adapter *(page 102)*. Coat the threads of the vent with petroleum jelly to ensure an airtight fit, and screw the vent into the adapter. Slip a female adapter fitted with an adapter for flexible pipe into the bottom of the T. Slide the main drainpipe over the adapter and clamp it fast.

Natural Cold Storage: The Root Cellar

Before building the most famous of all America's woodland retreats, at Walden Pond in 1845, naturalist-philosopher Henry David Thoreau dug a root cellar to preserve his crops through the winter. Thoreau dug his cellar "in the side of a hill sloping to the south, where a woodchuck had formerly dug his burrow, down through sumach and blackberry roots, and the lowest stain of vegetation, six feet square by seven deep, to a fine sand where potatoes would not freeze in any winter."

Today, more and more people are rediscovering the technique of storing crops underground to preserve them. Thoreau's root cellar was like those built today in both size and location—about 7 feet deep and 6 feet square and located at the cold north side of a cabin. Modern root cellars like the one shown below can be shored with grouted masonry blocks or with pressure-treated timbers. A set of steps and a hinged trap door complete the cellar. A floor of moist compacted earth will help maintain the 80 to 90 per cent humidity that helps to preserve food.

"In almost all latitudes," Thoreau wrote, "men dig into the earth for an equable temperature." As a general rule, root cellars can be used wherever the ground is cold enough to keep produce between 32° and 40° throughout the winter. In areas with a high water table, root cellars must be built aboveground, with soil banked around three sides. All root cellars should be well-ventilated with a screened outlet, to prevent what one poet has called "a congress of stinks."

Simpler to make, and adequate for short-term storage of small amounts of produce, is a cone-shaped root pit. A hole 6 to 8 inches deep and 1 foot across is lined with a layer of straw or leaves. Vegetables or fruits—which should not be stored together—are stacked in a cone-shaped pile and covered with more bedding. The entire pile is topped with 3 to 4 inches of soil, but some bedding is extended out the top of the dirt for ventilation. The straw is covered with a short board, the soil is tamped so water will run off and a shallow drainage ditch is dug around the pit. Once the pit is opened, the entire contents should be removed.

Preparation of crops for underground storage is not simply a matter of sticking them in the ground; without proper handling an entire store of food can be ruined. As a rule, produce should be harvested as close to the first frost as possible. Traditionally, root crops are air-dried so the skins harden, and the tops are cut to within an inch of the crown. Beets, carrots and turnips can then be buried in damp sand and covered with a layer of straw. Potatoes must be stored in bins. Produce with a high water content—such as tomatoes and peppers—will not last beyond January; stored apples, dried beans, onions and potatoes are still edible in spring.

A Choice of Simple, Safe Disposal Systems

Even small amounts of refuse and waste water from a cabin or cottage must be disposed of with care—and by the method appropriate to the material. You must cope with a variety of different materials: the solid debris of day-to-day living, the liquids that drain from a sink, and the wastes of a toilet *(pages 119-121)*.

Many vacationers burn solid waste such as trash or garbage, or bury it in a remote trench. Others can dispose of their refuse at a local dump, and still others take it home in a plastic bag for pickup by a trash-collection service.

Waste water from a sink presents a different disposal problem. In all but the most remote regions, sanitary codes generally forbid the old-time practice of simply sloshing the contents of a wash basin on a handy patch of ground—and with good reason. Wash water is frequently high in phosphorus and grease, and may contain food particles, bacteria and viruses—substances that can pose a health hazard if they are not conducted safely away from dwelling places.

Before you design your own water-disposal system, consult local health officials, who will tell you the kind of system required in your locality. Some sanitary codes call for a full-scale septic system *(page 118)*, of the kind that is used with a flush toilet; others accept the smaller installations and simpler methods shown on these pages.

Any system you install must include a pretreatment tank, or grease trap, in which solids settle to the bottom and pipe-clogging greases float to the top before the water is dispersed by absorption or evaporation. Locate the trap at least 50 feet from the nearest well or stream, and at least 10 feet from both the cabin and the property line.

If you dispose of less than 10 gallons of water a day, a 30-gallon plastic garbage can makes an ideal grease trap *(page 118, bottom left)*. For disposal loads between 10 and 50 gallons daily, use a precast concrete distribution box *(page 118, bottom right)* in addition to the grease trap; the box supplements the action of the trap, and also routes water to a larger absorption or evaporation area. Larger volumes of waste water require the use of a septic tank.

After passing through a trap or tank, waste water is piped away for final disposal, generally by absorption into the ground, which can soak up and filter waste water until the soil is saturated or, in technical language, overloaded. To determine whether overloading is likely in your area and under your disposal load, you must know the soil's capacity to absorb liquids. In many areas, suitable soils can be identified with the help of U.S. Department of Agriculture maps and reports, and the advice of the USDA extension service. Elsewhere, examination of the soil provides clues: as a rule, the best soils for drainage and absorption are light and sandy, and break apart easily into clods of uniform shape and size.

The final step in gauging the drainage characteristics of a soil is a percolation test, which in many areas must be performed by a sanitary engineer. The tester digs several holes on the site, fills the holes with water and measures the time it takes for the water to drop 1 inch. In general, the percolation rate for an absorption trench should not be more than 60 minutes per inch, though local authorities set their own standards.

In deciding upon the type of disposal system you must have, health officials consider the size and shape of the disposal area, the topography of nearby land, the amount of water to be handled and the percolation-test results. If waste-water volume is fairly light and the drainage capacity of the soil is good, you may get approval to build a simple seepage pit *(below)* or an underground disposal bed *(right, top)*. An evapo-transpiration bed *(right, bottom)* may be permitted in areas of high temperature, low humidity and poor drainage.

Four Basic Systems

A seepage pit. The simple stone-filled pit at right, which contains waste water until the water is slowly absorbed into the surrounding soil, is adequate for low-volume water treatment. Waste water flows down from the cottage in a 2-inch pipe and enters a small grease trap—in this example, a 30-gallon plastic garbage can *(page 118, bottom left)*. Solids settle to the bottom of the trap, congealed grease rises to the top, and the relatively clear waste water trickles through a pipe into a pit 4 to 7 feet deep.

The pit is filled with irregularly shaped rocks and topped with a mound of dirt; a 1- to 2-inch layer of straw or hay between the dirt mound and the rocks below it prevents earth from sifting into the spaces between rocks.

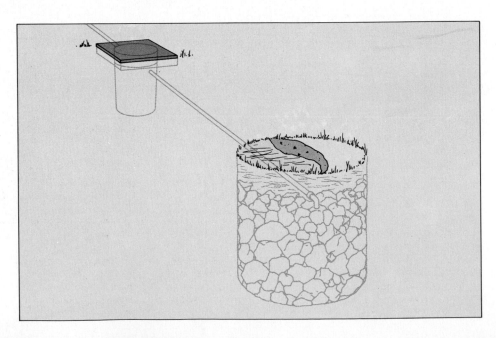

A network of underground pipes. In this disposal-bed system, waste water is distributed evenly through perforated pipes to the surrounding soil.

From a garbage-can grease trap, the waste water flows into a concrete distribution box, where its velocity is slowed by an internal baffle or wall in the box; the water is then channeled equally to 4-inch perforated pipes. Both the distribution box and the pipes are set level in a bed (at least 10 inches thick) of stones ¾ to 3 inches in diameter. Cover the pipes with at least 2 inches of stones, then add a 2-inch layer of hay or straw and an 8-inch mounded topping of soil.

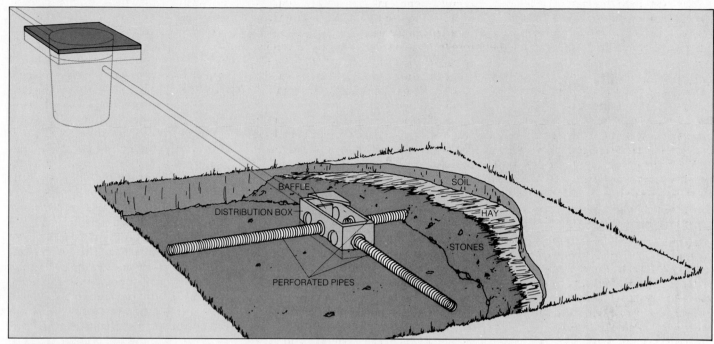

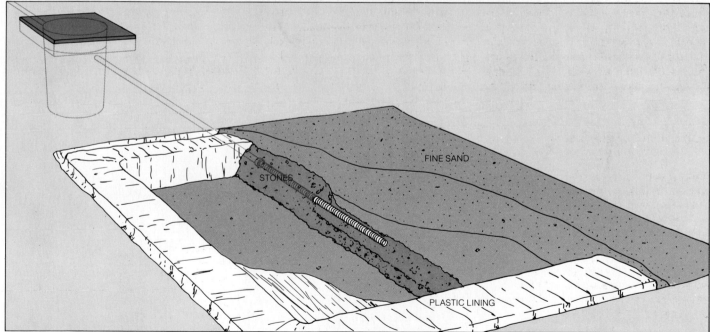

An evapo-transpiration bed. Between 1½ and 3 feet deep, this bed is lined with 10-mil plastic, to prevent water from seeping into the soil, and filled with fine sand. Waste water runs from a grease trap into a 2-inch perforated pipe that extends to the middle of the excavated bed; the pipe is surrounded by stones to prevent sand from blocking its perforations. Heavy waterproof tape is used to seal the area where the pipe enters the plastic liner. A bed that is used only during the summer can be seeded with alfalfa to speed the evaporation process. For the winter months, when periods of sunshine are brief, no vegetation should be planted.

Septic tank with absorption trenches. Waste water flows through an underground pipe to the septic tank, where solids sink to the bottom, oils and grease float to the top, and gas escapes back through the inlet pipe to the house drain vent. The remaining liquid, which is called the ef-fluent, flows slowly through the outlet pipe and out into a drainage field.

In this example, the drainage field consists of a closed loop of perforated pipes that releases the effluent downward and outward into the sur-rounding soil. The pipes are laid in level trenches, which may be 10 to 36 inches wide, 2 or more feet deep and 6 to 10 feet apart. They rest on at least 6 inches of stone, and are topped with 2 or more inches of stone, 2 inches of straw or hay and 4 to 6 inches of soil (inset).

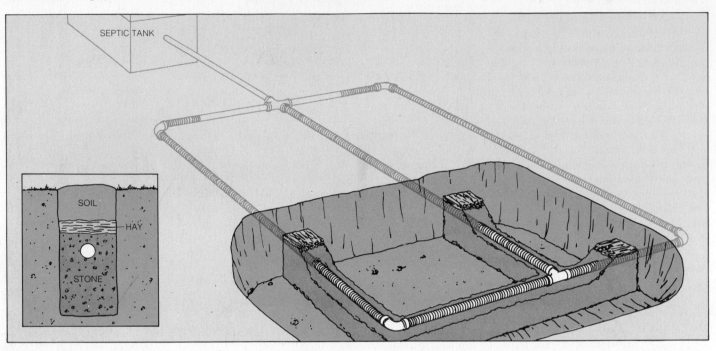

Connections at a Trap, Tank and Box

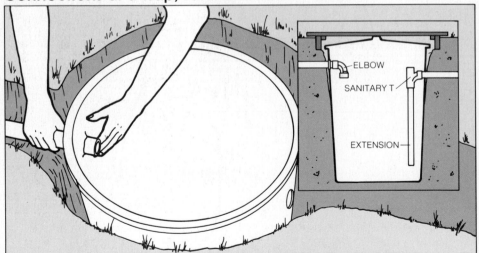

Making a grease trap. On opposite sides of a 30-gallon plastic garbage can, just below the rim, cut holes slightly smaller than the inlet and outlet pipes, with the inlet hole at least 1 inch higher than the outlet hole. Set the can in a level pit and pack the space around it with dirt up to the bottoms of the holes; dig trenches from the cabin to the inlet hole and from the outlet hole to a seepage pit or distribution box. Force the inlet pipe through the inlet hole, seal the hole around the pipe with silicone caulking and at-tach a 90° elbow, pointing downward, to the inner end of the pipe. Insert and seal the outlet pipe; at its inner end, attach a fitting called a sanitary T, connected to a pipe that ends at least 5 inches above the bottom of the can (inset).

Set the garbage-can cover in place, pack the re-maining space around the sides and conceal the can with a wooden cover. Inspect the trap periodically; remove large accumulations of grease and solids with a shovel and bury them.

Sealing a box or a tank. In disposal systems containing a septic tank or (as in this example) a distribution box, seal around the inlet and out-let pipes with mortar. Set the outlet pipes at the same level and the inlet pipe at least an inch higher to prevent the system from backing up (some codes require a septic tank inlet pipe to be 3 inches higher than the outlet pipe). Then fill the spaces around the pipes inside and out-side the box with chips of brick and apply a mortar of 60 per cent cement and 40 per cent sand.

Building a Traditional Country Privy

The old-fashioned outhouse or privy provides a comfortable, inexpensive alternative to the common flush toilet. Properly built, as a lined pit topped by a small structure for privacy, it will not contaminate surface soil or water supplies, and it will be virtually odor-free. Liquids seep slowly into the ground, gases escape through a ventilation pipe, and solids decompose in the pit. Depending on its construction and maintenance, the privy will be usable for 5 to 15 years.

Many local health officials will supply free advice and plans for locating, building and maintaining approved pit privies. Generally, they recommend locations downhill from a well and at least 50 feet from a house. The pit bottom should be at least 5 feet above the water table.

Outhouses should not be built on a flood plain or in an area containing fissured rocks or limestone formations that can carry pollutants to distant wells. Small depressions in slightly sloping ground can become waterways every spring, flooding a privy pit and causing it to overflow. In any location, soil quality is critical in the selection of a site. The ideal soil contains roughly equal proportions of sand, silt and clay; if there is too much sand, bacteria can spread over long distances; if there is too much clay, liquids will not be absorbed.

After selecting a site, dig the pit and build a lining *(page 120)*. A concrete floor over the pit will last indefinitely, but for occasional use, an easily built wooden floor *(page 120)* will do almost as well.

A privy's life span is determined in large measure by its maintenance. The better the balance of carbon and nitrogen in the pit, the more quickly wastes decompose—and the longer it takes for the pit to fill. To offset the high nitrogen content of human waste and to reduce odors, sprinkle wood ashes, straw, or sawdust into the pit after each use.

When the pit is filled to within about 18 inches below ground level, disassemble the house and move it to a new location; cover the old pit with a 2-foot mound of dirt.

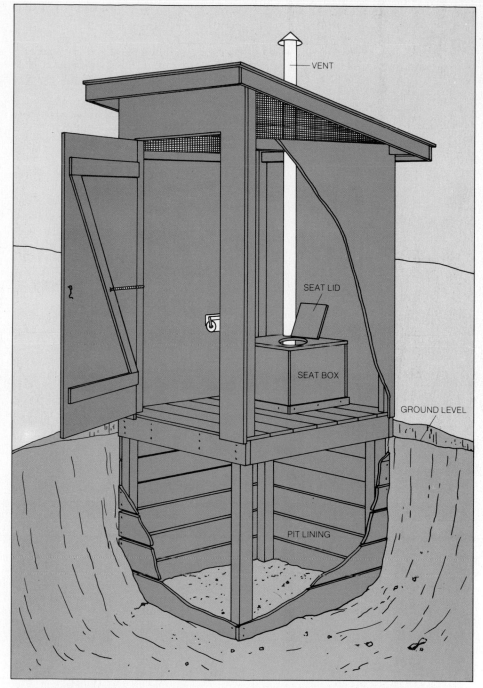

Anatomy of a pit privy. Dug by hand or backhoe, the pit above is square in this example; other designs are rectangular, and pits vary from 36 to 48 inches wide and from 3 to 7 feet deep. To prevent cave-ins during digging, the sides must be braced with plywood. For the finished pit, the lining should be made of lumber pressure-treated with a commercial preservative so the wood will withstand constant contact with the earth for several years. The wooden floor fits over the top of the pit lining and rests upon the ground. A seat box, built of 2-by-2s and plywood, fits into a hole in the floor and is held in place by 1-by-3 strips nailed to the box and the floor.

The seat hole is covered with a light, fly-tight lid. To ventilate the pit, a 4-inch stovepipe, screened and capped at the top, extends down into the seat box and up above the roof.

The sides of the privy house are framed with pressure-treated 2-by-4 columns secured to the floor; 2-by-4s are also used to frame a shed roof. Screened vents are left at the top of the structure, and a self-closing door is fitted into the highest wall. The entire building is tightly sheathed and roofed. To prevent ground water from reaching the pit, a well-tamped mound of dirt extends 2 feet from the floor level on all sides.

Finishing the Privy Pit

1 **Lining the pit.** After digging a square or rectangular pit, assemble an open-ended liner box 2 inches smaller than the pit in width and length and about 7 inches deeper, and lower it into the pit. To make the liner, use 4-by-4 corner uprights and side, front and back boards that are 1 inch thick; space the boards that will be more than a foot below the surface about ½ inch apart for drainage. In the top edges of the boards at the front and back of the box, cut out rectangles 1½ inches wide and 3½ inches deep, spaced at the width of the privy seat and equally distant from the center. Level the liner box, if necessary, by pushing it down into the bottom of the pit, and tamp dirt between the outside of the box and the pit walls.

2 **Framing and covering the floor.** Assemble a box frame of 2-by-8s 4 inches wider and longer than the liner box, with 2-by-4 braces, spaced the width of the privy seat and equally distant from the center, nailed between the front and back of the frame. Nail a covering of pressure-treated boards, 1 inch thick, over the frame, leaving an opening for the seat box. Set the completed floor on top of the liner box, with the 2-by-4 braces resting in the slots of the box and the frame resting on the ground.

Chemicals and Composting for Convenience

If you want the convenience of an indoor toilet, or if soil or water conditions prohibit the installation of a pit privy, chemical and composting toilets are practical alternatives to the outhouse. Just as for a privy, you must get the approval of your local health department before you make the installation.

Chemical toilets, designed to operate in all climates, are used by such government agencies as the U.S. Forest Service, National Park Service, and Parks Canada. For weekend cabin-dwellers, inexpensive portable models good for a maximum of 40 to 50 uses are available from camping-supply stores and mail-order houses. Though they are relatively odor-free and easy to use, they have one major disadvantage: their receptacles require frequent dumping, cleaning and refilling with a disinfectant. For longer periods of use, you may want a unit of larger capacity, such as a recirculating chemical toilet *(top, right)*, similar to the ones installed on a modern jet aircraft. Some of these units can be used up to 1,000 times before being emptied, and with an additional holding tank their capacity can be extended. Full tanks are emptied by special service trucks or owner-purchased portable pump-out tanks.

In a composting toilet *(bottom, right)*, human wastes are mixed with kitchen and garden wastes in a large container where they decompose into a rich fertilizer. Large, relatively costly commercial models require little maintenance, and have few moving parts that might break down; smaller and less expensive models need careful tending and require electricity for heating coils and fans to speed the composting process. Manufacturers provide complete instructions for installing and maintaining their units.

A recirculating chemical toilet. A foot-pedal flusher activates a pump that sends chemically treated fluid from a holding tank through the toilet bowl; the wastes are flushed back to the tank. At intervals recommended by the manufacturer, the tank is emptied, hosed down and refilled with water and chemicals.

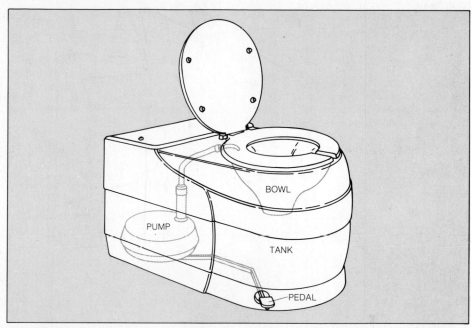

A composting toilet. Body wastes and garbage are deposited through the toilet stool to rest upon the inclined bottom of the composting tank. The wastes seep along a starter bed of peat moss and rich topsoil, while gases and evaporated liquids escape through a ventilation pipe. After about two years the waste turns into humus and is removed through an access door in the front of the container.

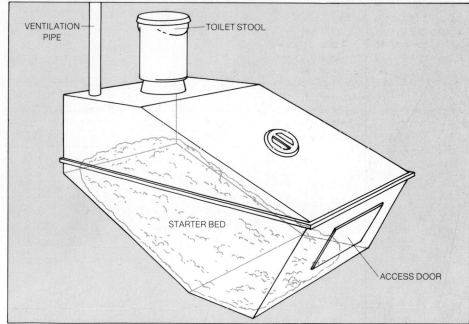

121

Stoves that Make a Little Wood Go a Long Way

In 1742 Benjamin Franklin boasted that his newest invention, a wood-burning stove, had the "advantage above every other method of warming rooms." Methods of home heating have changed since then but even today, after more than a century of central heating, variations of Franklin's open, cast-iron box provide a simple, inexpensive way of heating a room or a small cabin. Today's stoves burn coal as well as wood and come in a variety of sizes and shapes. Some nurse their burning logs as a smoker nurses a slow cigar, so that a single log lasts more than 20 hours. The best of them can heat a cabin for the winter with half the wood required by older, less efficient stoves.

The key to high efficiency is an airtight firebox. Here, in the main body of the stove, a metal sheet called a baffle slowly circulates the burning gases that account for more than 50 per cent of a wood fire's heat. As a result, the stove's surface temperature rises higher and the firebox radiates more heat.

Fireboxes come in sheet metal, plate steel or cast iron. Sheet metal, the least expensive, cools quickly when the fire dies, and tends to warp and to burn through when overheated. Welded plate steel holds heat longer, but it too tends to warp. Cast iron, the most expensive of the three, lasts longest, retains heat best and generally will not warp; it may, however, crack when overheated.

Above the firebox, stove parts are more or less standard. Most stoves come with enough stovepipe to reach an 8-foot ceiling; the insulated chimney pipe that runs through the ceiling must be purchased separately, along with a kit of fittings to support the pipe on the roof. Buy enough chimney pipe to meet minimum height requirements *(page 124, Step 4)*. You will also need flashing, a storm collar and a chimney cap to prevent downdrafts and keep rain out of the chimney.

If possible, locate the stove in the middle of the cabin for the best heating; in any location, it should stand at least 3 feet away from combustible wall material. If you place the stove closer than that to a wall, choose a location near the gabled peak to avoid the need for an unwieldy length of chimney pipe, and cover the part of the wall behind the stove with

fireproof reflecting material to protect against fire and help circulate heat. Whatever the location, protect the floor under the stove with asbestos millboard, bricks or a box of sand or gravel at least 2 inches deep, and extend this protective bed 1½ feet beyond all sides of the stove.

In operation, a high-performance stove creates one special problem—a coating of flammable creosote that collects on

the inside of the chimney. If allowed to build up, the sticky, tarlike coating may start a dangerous chimney fire. You can reduce the hazard by lighting a hot fire every day and keeping it going for 15 to 30 minutes to burn off the creosote in small amounts. If creosote deposits do build up, the chimney can be cleaned with special wire brushes or chemicals that are available from stove dealers.

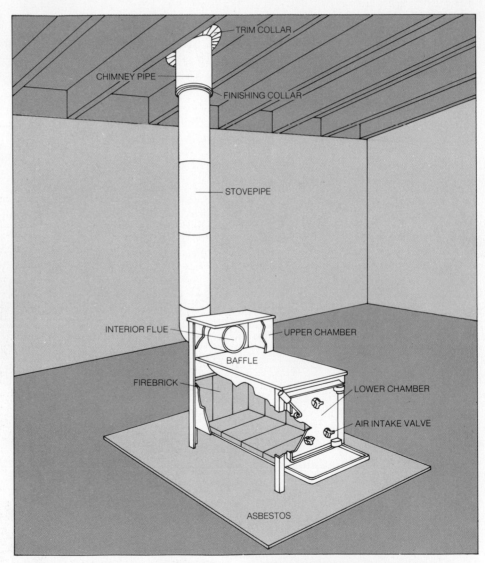

A high-efficiency stove. The installation of this modern wood-burning stove began with a sheet of asbestos to protect the floor. The stove itself consists of two chambers, with three air-intake valves in the door. Inside the firebox, firebrick retains heat for better combustion. A baffle at the top of the lower chamber forces burning gases to circulate fully. The upper chamber, fitted with an interior flue, further retards the escape of the gases into the stovepipe.

Above the stove, the stovepipe fits into a section of insulated chimney pipe that runs through a hole in the ceiling. A finishing collar seals the connection of the two pipes, and a segmented trim collar covers the edges of the ceiling hole.

Installing the Stove

1 **Marking the ceiling opening.** After running
sections of stovepipe from the firebox to within 18
inches of the ceiling, drop plumb lines from
the ceiling to the top of the pipe to mark the highest and lowest points where pipe will extend
through the ceiling, then mark the ceiling at four
additional points around the perimeter of the
pipe. Remove all the sections of pipe, cover the
firebox with cloth or plastic and drill pilot holes
through the ceiling and roof at each mark.

Subtract the stovepipe diameter from that of the
chimney pipe, add 2 inches for clearance and,
working on the roof, cut an ellipse in the roof to
this dimension beyond the pilot holes.

2 **Installing the chimney pipe.** Push the roof-
support section of chimney pipe down through the
hole you have cut until the support brackets lie
flat on the roof. Nail the brackets in place and add
one section of chimney pipe.

3 **Tying the pipes together.** Secure the finishing collar partway down the stovepipe with setscrews, then push the top of the stovepipe up into the chimney pipe and insert the bottom into the firebox. Loosen the setscrews on the collar, slide it up flush with the bottom of the chimney pipe and retighten the screws.

If the stovepipe and chimney pipe do not meet, add extra chimney pipe. If the stovepipe is too long, trim the top with metal shears.

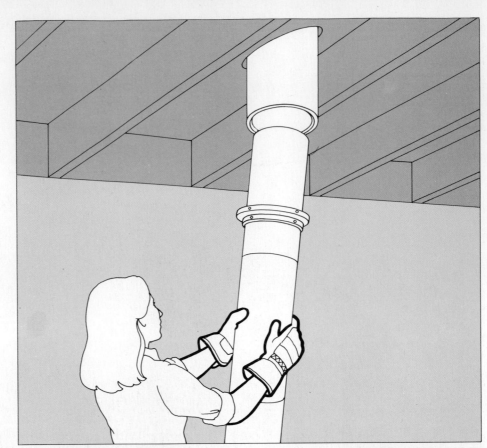

4 **Installing the flashing.** On the roof, spread a generous layer of roofing cement along the lines where the edges of the flashing will rest, slide the flashing down over the chimney and onto the cement and then nail the flashing to the roof. Cover the nails with a second layer of cement, spreading it over the edges of the flashing.

On a pitched roof, like the one shown here, add enough insulated pipe to extend the chimney 2 feet higher than any surface within 10 feet; on a flat roof, erect a chimney at least 3 feet high.

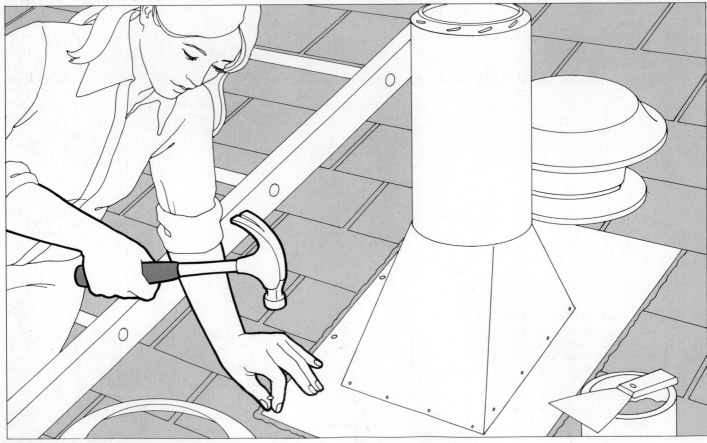

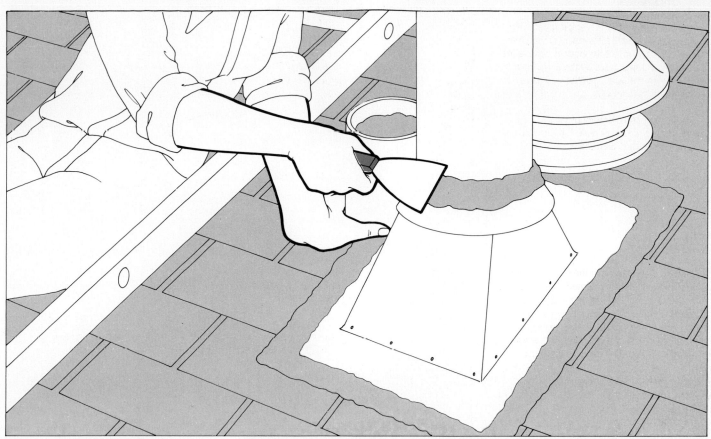

5 Putting on the storm collar. Fasten the storm collar around the top of the flashing and cover the crack between the collar and the chimney pipe with roofing cement. Add a chimney cap to the top section of chimney pipe.

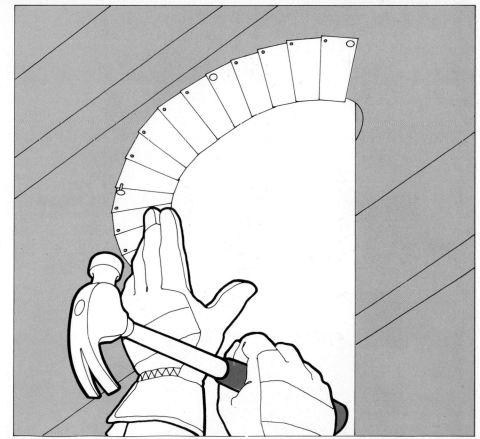

6 Putting on the trim collar. For easy fitting and installation, a trim collar comes in sections that resemble a necklace of aluminum rectangles, loose at the inner edges and fastened at the outer edges by open grommets; two or three sections may be needed to make a complete circle around a chimney pipe. To install the sections, arrange the loose edges around the pipe and flush to the ceiling; fasten the collar to the ceiling with ¾-inch nails in every fifth grommet.

Picture Credits

The sources for the illustrations in this book are shown below. The drawings were created by Roger C. Essley, Fred Holz, Judy Lineberger, Joan S. McGurren and Jeff Swarts. Credits for the pictures from left to right are separated by semicolons, from top to bottom by dashes.

Cover: Fil Hunter. 6: Fil Hunter. 9: Whitman Studio, Inc. 10 through 13: Peter McGinn. 14 through 25: Walter Hilmers Jr. 26 through 31: John Massey. 32: Adsai Hemintranont. 34: Fil Hunter. 36 through 43: John Massey. 44 through 51: Frederic F. Bigio from B-C Graphics. 52 through 63: Walter Hilmers Jr. 64, 65: Frederic F. Bigio from B-C Graphics. 66: The New York Public Library. 67 through 73: Frederic F. Bigio from B-C Graphics. 74 through 77: Peter McGinn. 78: Fil Hunter. 81 through 85: John Massey. 86 through 89: Frederic F. Bigio from B-C Graphics. 90 through 93: Gerry Gallagher. 94, 95: Forte, Inc. 96 through 99: Peter McGinn. 100: Fil Hunter. 102 through 105: Eduino J. Pereira. 106 through 112: Whitman Studio, Inc. 113 through 115: Forte, Inc. 116 through 121: Whitman Studio, Inc. 122 through 125: Raymond Skibinski.

Acknowledgments

The index/glossary for this book was prepared by Mel Ingber. The editors also wish to thank the following: Robert I. Abrash, Abrash and Eddy Architects, Reston, Va.; Marty Allen, Environmental Protection Agency, Cincinnati, Ohio; American Society for Testing and Materials, Philadelphia, Pa.; Glen C. Baker, Alexandria, Va.; John Baker and Tim Miller, Dempster Industries, Inc., Beatrice, Neb.; Dr. P. W. Basham, Division of Seismology and Geothermal Studies, Government of Canada, Ottawa, Canada; Charles E. Beatley Jr., Alexandria, Va.; Chris Beatley, Alexandria, Va.; Mark Beecher, MCC Clayton Mark, Lake Zurich, Ill.; E. R. Bennett, Department of Civil, Environmental and Architectural Engineering, University of Colorado, Boulder, Colo.; Priss and Woody Bernard, Portland, Ore.; Herman Blankenship, City of Alexandria government, City Shop, Alexandria, Va.; Donald Blevins, Virginia Concrete Company, Springfield, Va.; Kevin Callaghan, Dick Branham and Tom Redmond, National Concrete Masonry Association, McLean, Va.; Richard Brillantine, Fairfax, Va.; Betty Brush, Timber Lodge of Virginia, Washington, D.C.; Ken Campbell, Campbells Bottled Gas of Virginia, Inc., Alexandria, Va.; Donald L. Carr, National Association of Home Builders, Washington, D.C.; Wayne Cartwright, Occidental, Calif.; Curt Chandler, Ken Garvey and Nicholas Lally, Flood Plain Management Division, Federal Insurance Administration, U.S. Department of Housing and Urban Development, Washington, D.C.; Zandy Clark, Kennebunkport, Me.; Bob Collins, McNear Company, San Rafael, Calif.; Jack W. Deem, Deem Heating and Air Conditioning, Lorton, Va.; H. J. Degenkolb and Loring A. Wyllie Jr., H. J. Degenkolb and Associates, San Francisco, Calif.; Jim Devine, U.S. Geological Survey, Office of Earthquake Studies, Reston, Va.; Adrian Dioli, Sunnyvale, Calif.; Theodore J. Duke, American Wood Preservers Institute, McLean, Va.; ECOS, Inc., West Concord, Mass.; James P. Elliott, American Plywood Association, Tacoma, Wash.; Fairfax Tree Service, Fairfax, Va.; Richard Fernau, Berkeley, Calif.; Bill and Diane Fisher, Moyers, W. Va.; Gene B. Fox, Flint and Walling, Kendallville, Ind.; Sigmund Freeman and Peter Yanev, URS/John Blume & Associates, San Francisco, Calif.; Lelland L. Gallup, Department of Design and Environmental Analysis, Cornell University, Ithaca, N.Y.; Garden Way Publishing, Charlotte, Vt.; General Equipment Company, Owatonna, Minn.; David Glendinning, Monterey, Va.; Harry Goldman, Virginia Hardware Company, Arlington, Va.; Brian Gorman, National Oceanic and Atmospheric Administration, Washington, D.C.; David Graham, Lutherville, Md.; Bill Grant, Manassas, Va.; Jesse Haddon, Haddon Tools, McHenry, Ill.; Carl Hales, Northern Counties, Upperville, Va.; Hodge Hatfield, Alton Box Board Company, Alton, Ill.; Frances Hill, D. L. Bromwell, Alexandria, Va.; Tom Humphries, Ryan Homes, Richmond, Va.; Elmer E. Jones, U.S. Department of Agriculture, Beltsville, Md.; David Kirby, McCulloch Corporation, Los Angeles, Calif.; M. J. Kornblit, General Electric Company, Plainville, Conn.; Max L. Kroshel, Farallones Institute, Occidental, Calif.; Richard Kutina, American Gas Association, Cleveland, Ohio; George I. Lanham, Round Hill, Va.; H. E. Lloyd, Safe-T-Quake Corporation, El Monte, Calif.; Lawrence D. Martin, Pittsburgh, Pa.; Charles E. McIntosh, Generator Power Equipment, Inc., Bladensburg, Md.; William McKinney and James H. Lee, Monogram Industries, Inc., Long Beach, Calif.; Midwest Plan Service, Iowa State University, Ames, Iowa; Eugene Moreau, P.E., Division of Health Engineering, Department of Human Services, Augusta, Me.; Steven Moyer, Manassas, Va.; Patti Nesbitt, Strasburg, Va.; D. R. Norcross, Timber Engineering Company, Washington, D.C.; Northeast Regional Agricultural Engineering Service, Cornell University, Ithaca, N.Y.; Jim Painter, Dusty Reines and Lindsey Reines, Reines Motor and Trailer Company, Inc., Arlington, Va.; Steve Parsons, Dominion Well Company, Manassas, Va.; Norman Pollard, Mt. Vernon Tree Service, Alexandria, Va.; Powers Brothers Construction Company, Inc., Bristow, Va.; M. J. Rasmussen, New Mexico State University, Las Cruces, N. Mex.; James William Ritter, Springfield, Va.; Roland Wells Robbins, Lincoln, Mass.; Donald Schutte, Home Owners, Fairfax, Va.; Kenneth Semple and Mike Warnes, American Wood Preservers Institute, McLean, Va.; Sherwood Regional Library, Alexandria, Va.; Robert L. Siegrist, Small Scale Waste Management Project, University of Wisconsin-Madison, Department of Civil and Environmental Engineering, Madison, Wis.; Soil Conservation Service, U.S. Department of Agriculture, Washington, D.C.; Sonoco Products Company, Hartsville, S.C.; Southern Forest Products Association, New Orleans, La.; Bob Strunk, Commonwealth Tree Service, Arlington, Va.; U.S. Department of Housing and Urban Development/Federal Housing Administration, Washington, D.C.; Dale Vanderholm, University of Illinois, Urbana, Ill.; WACO Scaffold and Shoring Company, Beltsville, Md.;

Malcolm Walker, Sacramento, Calif.; Peter Warshall, Bolinas, Calif.; Edwin Wassil, Sentinel Valve Company, Paramount, Calif.; Jimmy Whitmon, Noland Company, Falls Church, Va.; Kirk Wilks, U.S. Activator Corporation, La Jolla, Calif.; Larry J. Wills, Virginia Frame Builders and Supply, Inc., Fishersville, Va.; Wood Research and Wood Construction Laboratory, Virginia Polytechnic Institute and State University, Blacksburg, Va.

The following persons also assisted in the writing of this book: James Randall and Warren Weaver.

Index/Glossary

Included in this index are definitions of many of the technical terms used in this book. Page references in italics indicate an illustration of the subject mentioned.

Pole necklace: *device to make possible narrow post holes.* Use, 80, *81*

Pole-frame cabin, 35, 64; building, 64, *65;* fastening beams to poles, *34, 35;* structure, *64*

Poles, wooden: cutting daps, *15;* digging holes for, 14, *15;* jacketing, 14, 15

Privy, 101, 119; building, *120;* siting, 119; structure, *119*

Rafters, 67; building for log cabin, 59, *60-61;* extending, *98;* for gable roof, 67, *69-71;* for shed roof, *67-68;* for snow regions, 97

Rebar. *See* Reinforcing bar

Refrigerator, gas-powered, 101

Reinforcing bar: bond beams, 90, 91, *92;* used in footing trench, 27, *28;* used in key wall, 80, *83;* used in masonry-block piers, 18, *21;* used in poured-concrete piers, *19;* used to reinforce foundation against earthquakes, 90, *91*

Reinforcing mesh, used in concrete-block wall, 28

Rocks, moving, 10, 13

Roof: building log-cabin, 59; erecting truss-type, *72-73;* extending for entryway, *98-99;* framing gable-type, 67, *69-71;* framing shed-type, *67-68;* pitch, 67, 74, 97; reinforcing for heavy snow, 96, *97;* reinforcing against wind, 86, *87, 88, 89*

Roofing: installing asphalt-shingle, *76;* installing 5-V crimp aluminum, *74-75;* installing shake, *76-77;* making shakes, *77;* materials, 74

Root cellar, *115*

Root pit, 115

Saw, chain: *See* Chain saw

Scaffold, for sloped site, *81*

Sink, installing, *114*

Slick. *See* Spud, peeling

Slopes, adapting a cabin to, 79, *80-85*

Snow, adapting a cabin for, 79, *96-99*

Spud, peeling: *tool used to peel bark from logs.* Described, *52*

Story pole: *board marked at intervals to align courses of masonry.* Use, 28

Stove, airtight wood-burning, 122; chimney, 122, *123-125;* cleaning, *122;* installing, *122, 123*

Thoreau, Henry David, 115

Toilets, chemical, 121

Trees: cutting saplings, 10; felling, *10-11;* felling away from lean, 10, *12;* felling deeply leaning, *12;* felling thick, *11;* moving logs, 13, 52; removing stumps, 13

Truss: *prefabricated component of gable roof.* Described, 72; erecting, *72-73*

Wall, key: *anchoring wall for foundation on sloped site.* Building, 80, *82-83*

Water: accessibility, 8, 100; driven wells, 101, 102, *105;* piping, 102; tapping rain water, 102, *103-104;* tapping surface water *102-103*

Water pump, electric: generator for, 9; jet, 106, *107-108;* submersible, 106, *109-112*

Water pump, pitcher, *100,* 101, *106*

Water pump, windmill, *113*

Wind: reinforcing cabin against, 79, *86-89;* temporary anchors for cabin, *89*

Windbreaks: fences, 79; vegetation, 79, 96

Windmill, *113*